WINDOWS & DOORS

Elizabeth Hilliard

First published in 1996 by
Conran Octopus Limited
37 Shelton Street
London
WC2H 9HN

This edition first published 1998

Text copyright © Conran Octopus 1996,1998
Design and layout copyright © Conran Octopus 1996,1998
The right of Elizabeth Hilliard to be identified as author of this Work have been asserted by them in accordance with the Copyright, Designs and Patents Act 1988.

All rights reserved. No part of this book may be reproduced, stored in a retrieval system, or transmitted in any form or by any means, electronic, electrostatic, magnetic tape, mechanical, photocopying, recording or otherwise without the prior permission in writing of the publisher.

Commissioning Editor: Denny Hemming

Senior Editor: Catriona Woodburn
Art Editor: Tony Seddon
Picture Researcher: Rachel Davies
Production Controller: Mano Mylvaganam, Jill Beed

Designers: Isabel de Cordova, Amanda Lerwill
Artwork Visualizer: Jean Morley
Illustrator: Clare Melinsky

British Library Cataloguing-in-Publication Data.
A catalogue record for this book is available from the British Library.

ISBN 1 84091 000 3

Printed in China

CONTENTS

Getting started 5

Decorative finishes for window frames and doors 10

Preparation for decorative finishes 12

Painting wood and metalwork 18

Finishes for woodwork 26

Special finishes on windows and doors 28

Finishing off 32

Curtains 36

Poles, tracks and accessories 40

Preparation for making curtains 44

Making curtains 50

Finishing touches 62

Blinds 66

Preparation for making blinds 70

Making blinds 72

Non-fabric blinds 76

Stockists and suppliers 78

Index 79

Acknowledgments 80

Getting started

Sashes, casement or dormers, panelled, flush or battened – the essential character of a home is to be found in its doors and windows. These important architectural features should never be allowed to fade into the background. Paint them in vibrant colours, or use finishes such as staining, varnishing and liming to bring out the beauty of bare wood. Choose from an exciting range of fabrics and accessories to create beautiful curtains and blinds that complement your individual style.

One of the wonderful things about windows and doors is that they are architectural. Good windows have structure and form which relate to the history of your home, its date and style. They genuinely have that often misrepresented quality, 'character'. Your windows may be things of beauty: elegant multi-paned Georgian sashes, Victorian with an interesting pattern of glazing bars, or rolled-steel casements original to an Art Deco house or block of flats.

Even a plain one-over-one Victorian sash, a row of pretty cottage casements or a handsome pair of modern wooden French windows can have proportions and an honesty of appearance which make the windows a pleasure to look at. Large plain windows in a contemporary building with a modernist or industrial look are equally attractive in a different way. Windows should be decorated in a decisive style which is sympathetic to, though not necessarily imitative of, their particular period and setting.

Doors, too, come in innumerable shapes, sizes and styles. Flush doors (a relatively modern invention) are flat on both sides. Panelled doors have recessed sections, often edged with moulding: two or six panels if Georgian or Georgian-inspired, four if Victorian or Victorian-inspired, three if early twentieth century. Cottage doors, made to varying degrees of sturdiness and sophistication from planks, the simplest usually being the oldest, are known as battened doors.

▲ *A modern flush door is painted a strong dusky blue, the same colour as the bedroom walls. The cylindrical steel knob reinforces the clean simple lines of this ex-workshop in London's Spitalfields. The radiator, painted to contrast with its background, becomes a feature rather than being disguised as one might expect.*

In spite of their significance and tremendous potential, windows and doors are often treated as the poor relations in a decorative scheme. Walls and floors are usually planned first, followed by the furnishings, while the windows and doors are thoughtlessly painted white or cream, or perhaps stained brown and varnished, and expected to merge into the background. This is not to say that in many circumstances white, cream or brown are not exactly the right colours. The point is that whatever colour and treatment you decide upon for your doors and windows, the choice should be a positive one, not a case of 'Oh well, white will do!'

Colour, even strong, vibrant colour, can look wonderful on the wood- or metalwork of doors and windows. It draws attention to them so that they make a greater contribution to the whole look of a room, perhaps reducing the need for elaboration elsewhere.

The original doors in your home are more likely than the windows to have been altered over the decades or centuries in response to changing fashions in interior decoration. Panelled doors were often simply covered on each side with a sheet of hardboard which can be removed and the door restored. If your doors are not consistent with the period of the house, or just do not look right for some other reason, you can simply change them.

Inappropriate flush doors may be replaced by panelled doors of the right size and period. These can be found in reclamation yards, bought new off-the-peg from DIY stores, or made for you by a joiner. Alternatively, you can make flush doors look like panelled doors, at a fraction of the cost of replacing them, by adding mouldings corresponding to the size and position of real panels.

Like doors, windows come in a variety of styles which reflect their history and sometimes their geographic location. A normal sash window has two panels, one above the other, one or both of which slide up and down. In some areas sashes are to be found which slide from side to side. The panes of sash windows are often subdivided by glazing bars, which generally add to their interest and charm.

The other most common window type is the casement, which swings open from one side. It is usually part of a series of similar-sized windows, some of which may be fixed in place rather than opening. Like sash windows, casements may be subdivided by glazing bars; a very old casement may be a leaded light, in which the divisions are strips of lead forming small diamond shapes. In a twentieth-century house a casement may be part of a metal window unit which includes a couple of fixed lights below a transom (a section which also swings open but is hinged at the top) alongside the casement.

◀◀ *In the charming inner hallway of an English country house, sage-green paint unifies several doors of different styles: one is a ledged and braced cottage door, one four-panelled, and the other has glass panes in its upper half.*

◀ *Large sash windows, painted plain white and uncluttered by curtains or blinds, make a strong contribution to the cool, airy atmosphere and pared-down look of this drawing room in a French country house.*

Other interesting window types include two which let light in through a roof. The dormer is a vertical window which with its housing breaks through the line of a sloping roof, usually in an attic room. A skylight or rooflight is usually overhead, following the line of the roof. The porthole is, as you would expect, a round window.

Windows are usually dressed with curtains or blinds. Practical and visually pleasing, they offer exciting opportunities for using fabric of almost every type, as well as rugs, blankets, saris and other purpose-made textiles.

Internal shutters are an often overlooked alternative to curtains and blinds. Handsome and clutter-free, they cut out draughts, noise and light with great efficiency, give a house added security and take up little space when folded open. Although curtains can be drawn across them at night, shutters can be splendid enough in themselves to require no cover-up. Sensibly, they are gaining popularity again.

▲ *Two pairs of dramatic, arched and glazed double doors allow light and (when open) fresh air to flood into a living room in Umbria in Italy. Outside, a simple iron balustrade across each window contributes to the modern look while also ensuring that the doors can be safely left open.*

You are fortunate if your house has its original folding or rolling wooden shutters, which may be nailed up waiting to be rediscovered. If the original shutters are missing, a joiner can be commissioned to make new ones, or you could make them yourself if you have the necessary carpentry skills.

There is, of course, no requirement for you to cover your windows at all. Shutters, curtains, blinds or anything else are used for a number of reasons, such as privacy, draught exclusion and visual appearance. But if a window has none of these requirements, and especially if it is well proportioned or looks out on a striking view of countryside or rooftops, leave it bare. This will be particularly effective in a room with a fresh, clear-cut, simple look.

Not all windows are situated in external walls or the roof, nor are they always see-through. A window in an internal wall gives

▲ *Tall sash windows in an eighteenth-century house would traditionally have had hinged shutters which folded back neatly during the day. When closed at night they excluded draughts and acted as a security measure. Nowadays, shutters can be made by a carpenter to fit almost any window – at a price.*

► *A simple, blue-framed dormer window, adorned only by a plain white roller blind, looks out over a pantiled roof and into the greenery of trees. Dormer windows push out through sloping roofs, allowing rooms in the eaves to receive adequate light, and also giving a little extra space and some non-sloping headroom.*

'borrowed' light to the room beyond. A glazed door does the same job; it might have been originally designed as such or it could be a traditional panelled door with some or all of its panels replaced with glass.

Plain clear glass is usually the obvious choice for most windows because it lets in the most daylight (which is, after all, the point of a window). But there may be windows in your home – on the stairs or overlooking a less-than-beautiful view, for example – where this need not be the primary consideration. A window which looks out into a dingy basement yard or other depressing sight, for instance, could be replaced with tough glass bricks which block the view while letting in plenty of light. (It is possible to have an interior, or even exterior, wall built using these bricks, which are usually associated with industrial buildings of the early twentieth century, to allow daylight into a room.) Alternatively, the clear glass of the window could be replaced with a type that you cannot see though.

▲ *Light floods through this renovated warehouse in Anvers, France, thanks to an expanse of metal-framed interior window which even has its own opening casements. Double doors are left bare on one side, painted white on the inside only. External windows are veiled with unbleached linen.*

Rooms such as bathrooms and lavatories call for glass which provides privacy, such as patterned glass. This could be embossed, where a raised pattern has been stamped onto the glass, or etched with a flat pattern. Etched glass is now manufactured in a variety of fairly traditional all-over designs. A plainer alternative is frosted glass. Where a window is in two sections one above the other, as in a subdivided casement or a sash, you can install frosted glass in the bottom half only for privacy and still get maximum light through the top. You can quite easily make 'frosted' glass to your own design using a self-adhesive plastic (see pages 30–31).

Yet another approach would be to commission an artist to design and make patterned glass which would be unique to your home. Alternatively, you could create your own design, perhaps incorporating your initials or something else with special meaning for you, and have it sandblasted onto a pane of glass by a local glazier.

Coloured panes and window shelves are two further assets you could use in planning the decoration of your windows. They can be used to create a degree of privacy or to mask a view, as well as for their intrinsic decorative qualities. You can either replace the existing panes with coloured glass or paint colour onto them (see page 31).

Window shelves - strips of toughened or laminated glass - are fixed like shelves across a window in the depth of the wall. Coloured glass objects look radiant exhibited there, or you could display a collection of items connected with the use of the room – shells and toy boats in the bathroom, perhaps, or antique cookery equipment in the kitchen.

Decorative finishes for window frames and doors

The technical advances made by big industrial paint companies, combined with the recent upsurge of interest in historical colours, traditional finishes, and in 'old-fashioned' and organic varnishes, stains and paint, have created a huge choice of materials with which to finish doors and windows in any decorative scheme.

An increasing number of specialist companies, most of which offer a mail-order service to customers, have nurtured the renewed interest in paints and interesting finishes from the past as well as the enthusiasm for organic products and natural finishes. Many small manufacturers are proud of their particular products, which include items such as biodegradable varnish and milk-based paints.

Before making a choice about the type of finish and colour you want for your doors or windows, it is well worth undertaking some research to find out more about the range of available products. The first step is to visit a well-stocked decorating shop, where you can read information on the paint cans and pick up manufacturers' information and colour cards. Also ask specialist suppliers for their product literature.

An option for stripped woodwork in good condition is to leave it bare or treat it with a protective varnish or sealant, or to nourish it with oil or wax (see pages 26–27), so that the natural beauty of the grain contributes a decorative element. If the colour of the wood is unsatisfactory in any way, it can be modified with the application of a wood stain (see pages 26). This can be a conventional 'wood' colour or a more brightly tinted shade to complement any overall colour scheme. Many stains are widely available in the usual DIY and decorating stores but some specialist companies make stains that can be diluted as much as you want to produce a washed-out look on wood.

Paint is the most wonderful stuff and it can be used in a number of ways to draw windows and doors into a decorative scheme. In addition to conventional painting techniques, special treatments can be applied to create different effects (see pages 19), including a distressed finish, in which previous coats of paint are allowed to show through worn-away areas, chips and scratches in the top coat.

Among so-called 'new' colours are many vibrant shades inspired by eighteenth- and nineteenth-century house decoration. These colours look magnificent on woodwork, emphasizing the architectural qualities of doors and windows. They are equally impressive whether the tone of walls and other features is pale, in which case they stand out, or strong, in which case colours on the woodwork add richness and variety to the overall look.

Some unusual modern paints which have caught the imagination of interior decorators can be used to create striking effects. Metallic-coloured spray paint, for example, was designed for re-touching exterior car paintwork but it can be applied in all-over swirls on a suitably primed door or with a stencil to create a pattern on doors or on fabrics for dressing windows. Paints designed for use on metal include all-in-one rust inhibitor, metal primer and top coat. They are easy to use and practical for metal windows and doors.

The choice of paint may have changed, but many of the old techniques for applying it have not. Whichever method you use, the aim is to have a smooth surface without blemishes at the end of the process. You could slap your paint on without any thought for technique, and as long as you work quickly and apply the correct thickness then the result will probably be perfectly satisfactory to the untrained eye. But the great attraction of techniques tested by use over a long time is that they work, and last (see pages 18–25). It is worth following them if you are serious about decorating because they are more likely than not to give good results with a minimum of fuss and mess.

Getting set up for decorating doors and windows involves little financial outlay. Compared to other decorating materials, paints, stains, oils and varnishes are inexpensive, though the cheapest is not necessarily the best; cheap paint contains extenders which fill up the can on the shelf in the shop but reduce its covering power at home. You do not need any special clothing (except for safety gear if you are using chemical strippers), just old, comfortable things which you do not mind getting splashed. The most expensive items are likely to be electrical equipment, such as a hot-air gun for stripping old varnish or paint, and a set of good-quality brushes. View these as an investment, to last you for many years.

▲ *A pair of Spanish-style wooden doors has a flower motif carved into each panel, and paintwork which is so distressed that it remains in only a few mottled patches. Doors bought from reclamation yards sometimes still have attractive layers of old paint.*

◄ *In this house belonging to a designer of woven textiles, the colour scheme uses old-fashioned paints in sumptuous colours from the English National Trust range: dead flat (matt) oil on the doors and woodwork, and estate emulsion (which has a chalky rather than a rubbery finish) on the walls.*

Preparing surfaces for decorative finishes

▲ *The doors and windows of this room have been painted with hard-wearing high-gloss oil-based paint. The better the surface preparation before painting, the smoother and longer-lasting the finished surface will be. In this case, the quality of finish is very important, as imperfections would be highlighted by the bold colour.*

How much preparation doors and windows require before they can be painted, stained or varnished will depend on whether they have been previously finished. What needs to be done to previously finished wood- or metalwork is dictated by the condition of the finish and what you want to cover it with.

The putty on windows must be sound before they are painted on the outside. Check the putty's condition before you paint and replace any that is dry, cracked or missing.

Discoloured patches in stripped woodwork can be bleached, as can large areas of wood that are an unsatisfactory colour, in preparation for a finish. Use specialized wood bleach, available from decorator's suppliers.

Preparing new wood

New wood requires relatively little preparation before paint, stain or varnish is applied. It must be clean and dust-free, however, as any debris will spoil the finish. Rough areas should be sanded and the dust wiped off.

Before new wood can be painted, the knots must be sealed with knotting solution to prevent them from seeping resin, which can stain the paint even after it has dried. It is a good idea to remove some of the resin before sealing the knots. To do this, apply heat using a hot-air gun to encourage them to weep, then wipe away the resin with a cloth soaked in white spirit. Apply the knotting solution with a small brush and wipe clean with methylated spirits. Two coats are ideal (it is quick to apply as it dries very fast), but one coat will suffice.

Preparing previously finished wood for painting or varnishing

If the existing finish is painted and in good condition, and door panel mouldings, architraves or glazing bars have clear edges and are not clogged with paint or varnish, wash the surface thoroughly with sugar soap or liquid sander (see page 15). Rinse well and dry. If you are not using liquid sander, lightly sand the surface with sandpaper or wet-and-dry abrasive paper wrapped around a cork block to create a key for the new paint to grip, and to soften the edges of any chips in the finish prior to touching them up with primer/undercoat. Bad chips may need filling and re-sanding. Always fill after the first coat of primer or primer/undercoat has been applied, as this helps the filler to grip.

If the existing finish is oiled or waxed, the wood will need thorough washing down before painting (see page 14).

Paint or varnish in poor condition will have to be completely stripped and the woodwork freshly primed and painted. Dry, flaky paint can be brushed off with a wire brush or dislodged with a scraper. The surface must then be sanded, with extra attention being paid to any stubborn patches of old paint. For large areas use an electric orbital sanding machine.

Hot-air gun: Thick, gungy paint that is clogging mouldings can be removed using a hot-air gun or by applying a chemical paint remover. If you use a hot-air gun, keep it moving along the wood to avoid scorching

Preparing painted surfaces

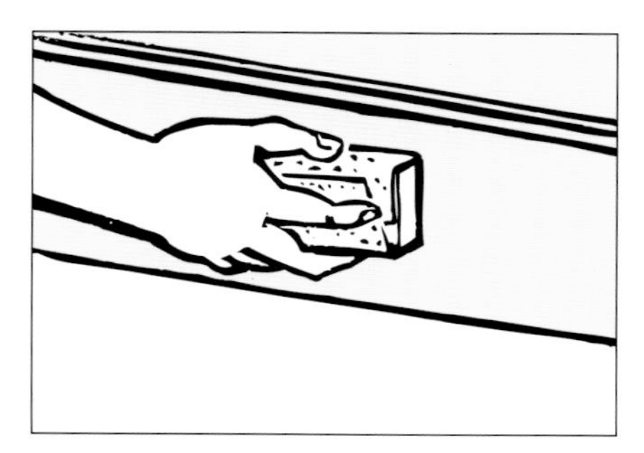

1 Use a sandpaper block to smooth surfaces and provide a key for painting. Work along the grain of the wood.

2 If the paint is hard to shift, or if large areas must be removed, an electrical orbital sander may be helpful.

and scrape off the melted paint immediately. Use a shavehook on any mouldings. Take care not to let hot paint fall on you. It may be advisable to wear cotton gloves for protection. Catch the scraped paint in a metal container such as an old baking tray and throw it away later, wrapped in old newspaper, in an outdoor bin, to prevent the possibility of fire indoors. When stripping glazing bars, add an attachment to the hot-air gun, with a rounded flat plate to one side, to protect the glass from the heat and the danger of cracking it.

Chemical paint strippers: Liquid and paste chemical paint strippers used in conjunction with scrapers and shavehooks are available for removing both oil- and water-based paint. On windows and doors use either a paste or a non-drip liquid or gel stripper. Other liquid strippers will, of course, run off vertical surfaces. Brush on the liquid and wait until the paint softens. Paste stripper is especially good for mouldings. Apply a thick layer and leave it for several hours. Once the stripper has had time to work, scrape and peel off the old paint and then wash down the surface. It is advisable to follow the manufacturer's instructions for application, removal, disposal of waste and, above all, safety to yourself. Paint strippers are necessarily corrosive, so protect yourself with goggles, gloves, and long-sleeved and long-legged workwear when using them, and keep the work area well ventilated. You may also need to wear a mask.

◀ Rubbing back old paintwork creates an attractive distressed finish you may decide you don't want to paint over. Sanding has created uneven, rough patches of colour on this door and table, giving them a convincing look of age which complements the colourwashed walls.

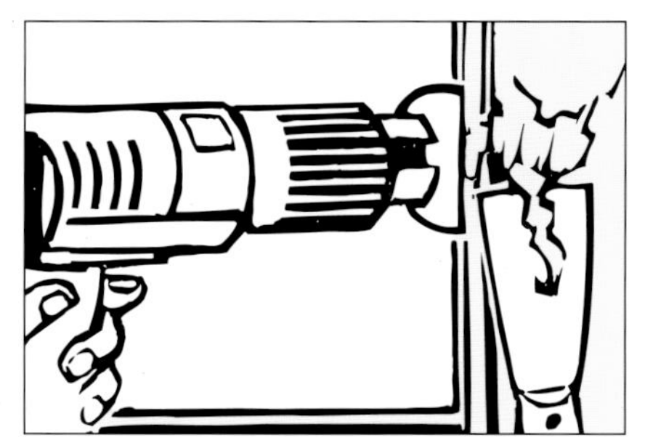

3 *A hot-air gun softens paint so that it can be scraped off. A heat deflector allows the gun to be used near glass.*

4 *Liquid stripper also softens paint. Brush it on, wait for it to work, scrape off the paint and wash the surface.*

5 *A paste remover is especially good for mouldings. Leave for several hours before peeling off, then wash down.*

Wood veneer and French-polished wood should never be cleaned in this way. Instead, use a specialist wood cleaner or, if the grime is superficial, wipe with a cloth dipped in a warm solution of water and malt vinegar, well wrung out so that it is barely wet. Wipe dry immediately.

Preparing new metal

Before painting new metal or finishing it with blacking, ensure it is completely dry and free from rust and grease. Rusty patches must be cleaned and cured with rust inhibitor before metal primer or paint is applied, unless you are using an all-in-one rust-cure paint.

▲ *The stripped pine sash windows and panelled window surrounds in this city bedroom help to create a clean, uncluttered feel. Their pale finish is emphasized by the milky whiteness of the limed floor, and is enhanced by the unlined calico curtains. Together, they provide a neutral background for the antique chair and bed.*

▶ *Rusty metalwork requires a fair amount of preparation before it can be painted: scrubbing down, cleaning, treating with rust killer and metal filler, and sanding. A little effort, however, pays dividends, and a smooth paint finish on a well-prepared surface can make once dilapidated metal frames look flawless.*

Preparing previously finished wood for staining

Because stain cannot penetrate paint, wood that has been painted must be completely stripped before stain can be applied; any overlooked patches of paint will give a blotchy and unsatisfactory result. Use a chemical stripper in liquid or paste form. To remove any stubborn patches of paint that may remain after the initial stripping, scrub along the grain using wire wool dipped in white spirit or, if you used chemical stripper, apply more of this.

Preparing previously finished wood for oiling or waxing

Before re-oiling, re-waxing or painting woodwork that has previously been oiled or waxed, clean it thoroughly to remove all the old waxy/oily deposits. Scrub the surface (not a veneered or French-polished surface) with steel wool dipped in white spirit, following the wood grain, then wipe down with a clean rag or paper towels. You may have to repeat this action several times. Finally, wash and dry the woodwork ready for treatment.

Preparing previously finished metal

If paintwork on metal window frames is in good condition it can be repainted with relatively little in the way of preparation. Just wash it with sugar soap or a solution of soda crystals, rinse and dry. Then sand the paint lightly, with fine sandpaper wrapped round a cork block, in order to create a key for the new coat of paint. Before starting to paint, thoroughly clean off any dust.

If the paintwork is in poor condition, however, it will require considerably more work before it can be repainted. Be sure to protect your eyes with goggles before brushing off all the loose material – rust as well as paint – using a sturdy wire brush. Next, scrub the metal with a solution of sugar soap or soda crystals, and rinse. Wipe down the entire surface with white spirit on a clean rag to remove any remaining grease. When it is thoroughly dry, paint rust killer onto bare or rusty patches, paying special attention to ensure it thoroughly permeates fixing boltheads, hinge areas and joints. When this has dried, fill holes and depressions in the framework with metal filler. Allow this to dry, then sand all over to create a smooth, even surface for painting. If priming the surface first, use a primer formulated specifically for metal which contains rust inhibitor.

Alternatively, strip off the old paint completely using a chemical paint stripper suitable for metal, and wire wool. A hot-air gun is of no use when stripping paint off metal, as the heat is absorbed by the metal, and the result is to bake the paint on.

Tools and equipment

The preparation of doors and windows for a new finish requires little in the way of specialist tools and equipment. In addition to the items described below you will need a screwdriver for removing ironmongery and door furniture before starting work.

- **Knotting solution:** an oily sealant made from shellac and methylated spirit which is painted onto the knots in new timber, especially pine, to prevent them weeping resin (see page 12), which can stain a paint finish.
- **Sugar soap or soda crystals:** washing existing paintwork with sugar soap or old-fashioned soda crystals dissolved in hot water is a marvellous way of removing dirt and grease, and even decades of caked-on grime.
- **Liquid sander:** a solution for cleaning surfaces prior to applying a new finish. It is particularly useful for cleaning and smoothing intricate mouldings and corners.
- **Sandpaper or abrasive paper:** essential at every stage of preparation to feather the edges of cracked or flaked paint or varnish; to create a key on existing finishes ready for the next one; to smooth and level dried filler after application; and between new coats of paint for a really glossy result.
- **Wire brush:** extremely useful for removing flaky paint and rust from metalwork.
- **Hot-air gun:** the cleanest, neatest and, some say, the safest way to strip paint is using a hot-air gun. Shaped rather like a hairdryer, this machine melts paint, even layers deep, which can then be scraped off with a scraper or shavehook. Some have integral scrapers and heat deflectors which allow paint to be stripped near glass. When it is fitted with an attachment shaped to channel the heat away from the panes, it is an ideal tool for stripping paint from glazing bars of windows. Never pass your hand in front of a hot-air gun to test how hot it is, as it will burn.
- **Shavehook:** a triangular tool for scraping narrow surfaces. The type with curved edges is designed to be used on the curved profiles of mouldings and glazing bars.
- **Chemical paint stripper:** powerful paint strippers can be used for removing paint. Special strippers are available for stripping paint off metal windows. Use these with wire wool. Whatever type of chemical paint stripper you use, whether a paste or a liquid, always protect eyes and hands. Cover arms and legs, however warm the weather, and carefully follow the manufacturer's instructions for safe storage and disposal of chemicals.
- **Rust killer:** preparations can be painted onto metal windows and doors where rust has pitted the metal. Clean the areas to be treated of all rust and paint on the solution. Fill the crevices with metal filler to create a smooth surface before painting.
- **Filler:** often necessary when renovating wood or metal to repair damaged surfaces. It is normally applied after the priming stage. Use the right sort of filler for the material you are working on. If mixing a filler up yourself, rather than using a ready-mixed type, be sure to add thinner in exactly the correct proportions, as directed by the manufacturer.

Preparing to paint

▲ *Narrow double doors are useful for dividing two rooms which interconnect and are often used together, as they look more welcoming and create less of a barrier when open than a single, full-sized door. Here, a panelled effect is suggested with roughly applied white paint.*

To work out how much finish you need to buy, measure the surface area of your windows or doors to get a rough idea of the area that needs to be covered, and check the estimated coverage details on the cans. Check, too, whether the finish requires any treatment: for instance, some paints are sold in a slightly concentrated form and need to be thinned with white spirit or other thinner before application.

Most are applied with brushes although some, such as stains, can be put on with a cloth. It is worth having a few improvised tools to hand in addition to the necessary decorating tools. An old spoon, for instance, is useful for lifting paint-can lids, especially ones that have been resealed for a few days.

Equipment choices for different paint effects

Always buy the best brushes you can afford, preferably natural fibre and ideally pure hog's bristle. Check that each brush is well made, with no loose parts and with a solid pad of flexible, springy bristles. You need a selection of paintbrushes for different jobs. Another point to remember is always to use a brush of the appropriate size: one that is too big will not get the job done any more quickly. For painting windows and doors you will need a 2.5cm (1in) decorating brush for mouldings, a similarly sized cutting-in brush for glazing bars, a 5cm (2in) brush for flat areas on panelled doors and a 7.5cm (3in) one for flush doors. Look after your brushes properly and they will last for many years.

For creating decorative effects with a glaze, brushes in different sizes will be useful. They are used dry. A bristle grainer, for example, is invaluable when dragging (see page 19), and a wallpaper-paste brush can be used to soften up lines. Combs are used for patterning glaze. These can be bought, made of steel or rubber, but can be customized easily from cardboard. For an even effect, cut the teeth evenly across the comb, or to create a freer effect, cut less symmetrical teeth. Rubber rockers for patterning a wood grain are like curved rubber stamps and are, quite literally, rocked over and through tinted glaze to produce *faux bois* finishes.

Lining brushes are useful investments for ensuring a stable flow of paint over a long distance and are especially suitable for painting *faux* panels. Sable and polyester lining brushes are best used for thin washes; try ox- and hog-hair ones for thicker paints. Sword-liner brushes have bristles that taper away to a point and these brushes are used for such effects as marbling, lining and detailed work.

Paintbrushes must be dry and clean before you begin a job. If a brush is new, work it against your hand to encourage the loosest bristles to drop out. More loose bristles can be removed by dipping the brush in water and then painting this onto newspaper or a rough surface such as an outside wall. Next, wash the brush throroughly in warm soapy water, rinse well and squeeze out most of the water. To speed drying, spin the brush between your hands before suspending it with its bristles hanging downwards.

When you buy your brushes, drill a hole through the wide part of each handle (not through the metal) large enough to take narrow-gauge dowelling. Cut sections of dowelling long enough to sit on top of a jar and to extend each side so you can store the brushes suspended from the dowelling with their bristles hanging downwards when not in use (see page 33).

▲ *Wide double doors look majestic when closed and create a generous, welcoming space when open. These examples have been painted in two colours, grey on the frame and mustard on the panels, both drawn from the curlicue pattern painted on the walls.*

Cleanliness

Cleanliness is important when applying any finish. When wet or tacky, surfaces can act like magnets to dust and dirt, which will spoil the final finish into which you have put so much effort. So even if you think your doors and windows are already clean, wipe them down again with either a clean cloth that is barely damp or a tack rag immediately before beginning decorating. Remove dust from the crevices of mouldings on doors and windows after sanding filler or paint. A vacuum cleaner with a brush attachment is useful for this.

To prevent dust and pieces of dried finish, especially paint, dropping into the can when you open it, clean the can before removing the lid, brushing loose bits out of the rim. If debris does fall in or if paint has formed lumps, strain the contents of the can through a piece of fine cotton muslin stretched over another clean container. Always remove the skin on paint, however thin; do not be tempted to work it into the paint in the hope that it will disappear.

Cloths and neat rags without trailing threads are useful for wiping up spillages and drips but they must be clean to avoid transferring dirt onto fresh paintwork. Tack rags, for wiping surfaces clean, can be bought from DIY or decorating stores.

Protecting yourself and your furnishings

Lay protective sheeting everywhere, even where you think splashes will never reach. Fine plastic sheeting is impermeable but can be slippery and cannot be satisfactorily repaired if torn. Decorator's fabric sheeting, used by professionals, is available in sheets of various sizes and weights.

It goes without saying that you should wear old clothes; they are going to get splashed with paint. Do not wear wool, as wet paint will pick up the fibres. To protect your hands during decorating work, it is worth using special protective handcream, available from decorator's suppliers. This gets into creases and cuticles and is as effective a barrier as wearing gloves, but with none of the disadvantages. You simply wash it off when you have finished painting, leaving cuticles and creases clear and clean.

Using paint

▶ *There is no paint so shiny and hard-wearing as good quality oil-based gloss. The deep-blue gloss used in this country-style kitchen-cum-dining room is practical as well as decorative; it can be wiped down and will withstand the onslaughts of dirt and condensation.*

Paint on woodwork

Both oil- and water-based paint can be used on woodwork. Traditionally, bare wood is prepared for top coats of paint with both primer and undercoat. Primer seals the wood and smoothes any slight blemishes. Undercoat, which can be coloured, gives a solid ground for the first top coat. All-in-one primer/undercoat is popular. The acrylic form dries quickly and can be painted over with oil-based paints as well as water-based ones.

Paint on metal

Metal requires special primer, filler, paint, thinner and cleaner. It is best to use products from the same brand. The more specialized paints do not need undercoat, and have rust-proofing qualities. They also need only one coat for complete coverage. For a really chalky, matt black finish on metal, consider using blackboard paint.

Applying paint

Paints need to be stirred thoroughly with a clean implement before use. A piece of wooden dowelling is ideal. However, do not stir non-drip paint or it will lose its non-drip qualities. If you do so in error, cover and leave the paint for several hours to stabilize.

Working with a heavy can of paint can be difficult and dangerous. Decant a proportion of the paint into a smaller paint kettle, or a clean metal or plastic container with a handle.

Loading the brush

Dip the end third of the bristles in the paint. A length of string stretched across the top of a paint kettle is useful for removing the excess. You need enough paint to work with, but not so much that it will dribble or form wrinkles as it dries. Read the instructions on the can for any additional advice about the particular paint you are using.

Paint choices

Oil-based gloss: Tough, hard-wearing and shiny, oil-based gloss paint is best applied in several thin coats (a minimum of two) rather than one thick one. Drying time is 12–16 hours although it may take several weeks, depending on the weather, for the paint to harden completely.

Oil-based silk: Oil-based silk paint has a smooth, silky finish that is not as shiny as full gloss paint. It is made by most industrial manufacturers but is given different names according to the brand. Drying time is 12–16 hours.

Oil-based eggshell: Oil-based eggshell has a smooth, hard-wearing surface and a slight sheen. It gives a more elegant finish than gloss. Drying time is 12–16 hours.

Flat oil: Also known as dead flat oil, it has a chalky, totally matt finish. Until recently it was considered to be exclusively a professional paint. Now more readily available from specialist paint companies, almost all of which offer a mail-order service, rather than from regular DIY or decorating stores. It is well suited to the woodwork of doors and windows. Drying time 6–12 hours.

Water-based (acrylic) gloss: Although not as brilliant as oil-based gloss, acrylic or water-based gloss paint has other advantages. It does not smell strongly, it dries quickly and it gives a good shine. It can be painted on more thickly than oil-based gloss, but needs immediate working out as it dries rapidly. It is easy to wash off hands and brushes with water and soap.

Whatever type of paint you choose to use, the way you load your brush and apply the paint can make all the difference to your technique and the finished paintwork. Avoid painting doors and windows during hot and humid weather, as the paint will not dry properly and there is a likelihood of moisture becoming trapped between coats to cause problems later on (see pages 32–33).

Applying paint

1 *Dip the lower third of the bristles in the paint, and wipe off excess on string stretched tightly across the paint can.*

2 *Paint three downward strokes, parallel but not touching, in the same direction as the grain of the wood.*

3 *Without reloading the brush, work over the strokes to spread the paint, at right angles to the original direction.*

4 *Finish by lightly 'laying off' in the original direction, to remove any brush marks and leave a smooth surface.*

First brush-strokes

Start painting at the top. On flat areas, first apply three downward strokes of paint, parallel with each other but not touching and painting along the grain. Without reloading, work over these downward strokes crossways to spread the paint, until it forms a solid block of colour.

Finish by 'laying off' in the original downward direction, with the grain of the wood, gliding your brush lightly over the surface. The point of laying off is to remove any marks made by the bristles of the brush, leaving a smooth surface. Reload and paint further sections in the same way, blending the paint over adjoining sections.

Special paint effects

Special paint effects can be applied to the woodwork of doors and windows to bring further interest to otherwise plain paintwork. Effects such as dragging, combing and woodgraining are achieved using a choice of tools, from decorating brushes to special rubber rockers, in order to pattern a further layer of paint or glaze over a base coat of oil paint.

Apply a base coat and leave it to dry. Tint transparent scumble glaze, mixing 1 part glaze to 3 parts white spirit. Add 1 part white oil-based eggshell per 20 parts of glaze; and add artist's oil paint to add colour. Mix up enough for all the woodwork you want to cover. While the glaze is still wet, lightly drag a wide decorating brush over the surface.

Dragging involves just that: dragging a decorating brush such as a bristle grainer through the top layer of tinted glaze so that the patterning of the brush strokes remains visible when dry. Combing with a special wide-toothed comb is particularly effective, if a substantial proportion of the tinted top coat is combed away, allowing a contrasting coloured undercoat to show through.

Woodgraining may be done using a special rubber rocker patterned with a woodgrain effect or, for a more impressionistic effect, using a lining brush to pull thin distressed lines over the base coat in a pattern similar to the veining of marbling. The technique for using the rocker is first to rock and then to gently drag it through the glaze.

Dragging

1 *Apply glaze over the base coat, then drag a decorating brush through it to leave a brush-stroke pattern.*

2 *Follow the direction of the grain roughly or the effect may be too mechanical.*

▲ *A top, coloured glaze wash can be dragged, as here, or treated using a range of other techniques – including combing and woodgraining – to create subtle paint effects. The soft colour combination of blue over cream on this cupboard door makes a clear visual link between the woodwork and the marble splashback behind.*

Painting windows

Painting a window is a fiddly job that should not be rushed, yet it needs to be done in one session to avoid ugly joins in the paintwork. Start early in the day and leave the window open so that the paint will be dry enough to close the window at night; do not attempt to paint in windy weather as dust will blow onto the wet paint and spoil it. Immediately before starting work, remove handles, stays and catches and clean the panes thoroughly so that dust or dirt cannot transfer onto the wet paint.

Applying the paint

If you are using an oil-based paint, remember to build up the paint in layers, beginning with a wood primer, progressing to an undercoat and then finishing off with one or two layers of top coat. Use a 2.5cm (1in) brush for flat areas and a cutting-in brush, which has an angled tip for painting mouldings and glazing bars, of the same size. Apply the paint downwards, along the grain if painting wood. Without reloading the brush, lightly work over this, making sure that paint (but not too much) gets into all the grooves of any mouldings. Finally, glide the brush down again, ensuring that the paint on all the surfaces is smooth and even.

Protecting glass

To protect window panes from paint, either use a paint shield or stick decorator's or masking tape on the glass close to the glazing bars or frame. Whichever method you use,

▲ *A dramatic use of colour draws the eye: vibrant blue on the wall and emerald green on the window. Despite having been built up in layers, the paint around the window has become worn with age, but far from offending the eye, this softens the brash green and adds to the window's charm.*

Painting around glass

1 *A paint shield is invaluable when painting window frames, to avoid getting paint on the glass.*

The painting sequences for casement and sash windows

1 To paint a casement window, follow the numbers, painting the opening windows first.

1 To paint a sash window, first reverse the position of the sashes, then follow the numbers.

let your paint overlap onto the glass by about 1mm (1/16in) to seal the join between glass and frame and protect it from damp.

A paint shield is a piece of shaped metal or plastic with a fine edge along one side. While you paint, you hold the fine edge against the glass, almost touching the glazing bar or side of the window. When using a paint shield, wipe it frequently to prevent it causing smears.

Stick masking or decorator's tape around the edge of the glass close to the wood. Wide decorator's tape, which is half self-adhesive and half plain paper, is the easier tape to remove when painting is complete. Peel away the tape before the paint has dried, otherwise it may take some paint with it.

Sash windows

Begin by reversing the window positions so that the bottom sash is pushed up and the top sash is pulled down. Paint the meeting rail and the vertical bars of the outer sash as far as is possible. Next, paint the area beneath the inner sash and the runners. Following this, paint the lower cross-rail and the underside of the inner sash. Leave to dry. Reverse the window positions and start by painting the upper cross-rail of the outer sash, and then the remainder of the vertical bars of the outer sash. Now paint the upper cross-rail of the inner sash, the vertical bars of the inner sash and finish off with the top runners and behind the cords, the frame and sill.

Casement windows

Fix the window open with a piece of wire wound around a nail tapped into the bottom of the opening casement. First paint the glazing bars and rebates, next the upper and lower rails, then the hinge stile and the window edge. Follow with the outer stile, and finally the frame and sill.

Shutters

Because of their similarity to doors, treat shutters as if they were a panelled door, taking care to wedge a whole shutter open before you start work. Leave the window itself open (unless it is windy) to help the paint dry.

▲ *This roomy colonial interior boasts an abundance of divided louvred shutters. They are ideal here, behind the desk, where their versatility can be exploited to advantage. One half of the shutters can be closed to shade the eyes while air and sunshine can still stream in above or below to refresh and inspire the mind.*

Painting doors

Like windows, doors should be painted in one session to avoid leaving visible joins in the paintwork. Remember that, as with all decorating, you will be able to see your handiwork more clearly in natural rather than artificial light. Cover the floor underneath a door and wedge it open firmly so it won't wobble as you paint. Before getting down to work, remove knobs, handles, catches, escutcheons, fingerplates and any other ironmongery. Have an old screwdriver handy for cleaning out the groove of hinge screws after painting them.

Paint the edges of a door outwards, towards the corners, to prevent paint being drawn off by the corners of the wood and running down in dribbles. On panel doors use a 5cm (2in) brush for stretchers and a 2.5cm (1in) brush for mouldings. For a flush door a 7.5cm (3in) brush is suitable.

▲ *Panelled doors provide a good opportunity for having fun with colour. Here light- and dark-blue paints have been used to make a striking entrance to the room. In times past, the panels were painted in slightly different tones of the same colour to provide a subtle sense of depth.*

Furniture

Metal fittings should be cleaned (see page 35) and coated with an appropriate paint, always making sure that moving parts and screw holes are not clogged.

Wooden door knobs, especially cupboard knobs, can be painted to match a colour scheme. Use a hard-wearing paint such as oil gloss or enamel, apply several thin coats and consider a final coat or coats of yacht varnish to help protect them from wear and tear.

Panelled doors

Always working with the grain, first paint the mouldings around each panel, then the panels themselves. Next paint the centre stiles, the cross-rails including those above and below the panels. Now paint the stiles down each side of the door, then the edges, and finally the door casing (jamb and door stop, and architrave) if these were not painted at the same time as the skirting board. When you paint the outside edges of the architrave use a paint shield (see pages 20–21) to prevent paint getting on the wall.

An old-fashioned technique for painting panelled doors is to use slightly different tones of the same colour on different parts of the door. By painting the panels the darkest shade, the frame the lightest and the mouldings a shade in between, the architectural features of the door are made more noticeable. The door looks like a three-dimensional object rather than a two-dimensional one.

Flush doors

The best way to paint the large flat expanse of a flush door is to mentally divide it into six or eight equal parts, two across and three or four down, rather like the sections in a bar of chocolate. Start by painting the top left section, then the top right, then the next left, then next right, and so on down to the bottom of the door. Paint each in turn, blending the wet edges together as you work down the door. Paint the edges, jamb and architrave as for panelled doors.

Flush doors can offer greater and more varied opportunities than panelled doors for extravagant painting styles. Their flat sides

The painting sequences for panel and flush doors

1 For a panelled door, start with the mouldings around the panels, and then follow the sequence of numbers.

▲ *The frame of a metal glass-panelled door is painted black, drawing attention to its geometric design. The squareness of the panels contrasts pleasingly with the generous curve of the red-painted wall in front of the door. Glass blocks above this wall serve to create an internal window as well as echoing the panels of the door.*

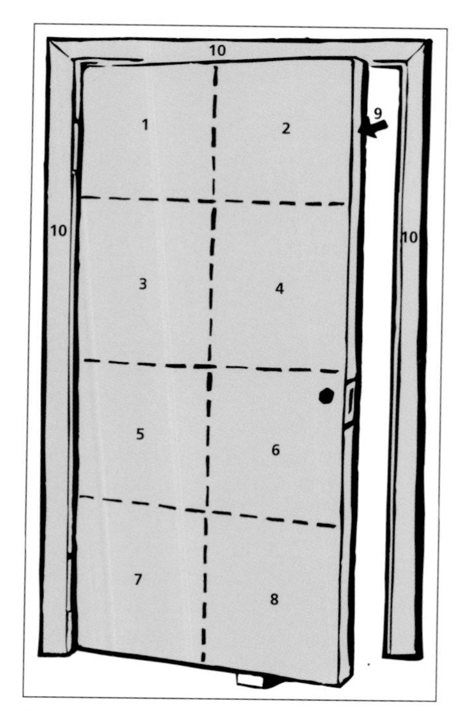

1 Work down a flush door from the top in imaginary sections, blending wet edges together before they dry.

lend themselves to all-over designs such as the eye-bending geometric patterns found in the work of pop artist Bridget Riley or the blown-up cartoons of Roy Lichtenstein. Some of the most famous examples of door painting can be seen at Charleston Farmhouse in Sussex, where the artists Vanessa Bell (Virginia Woolf's sister) and Duncan Grant used every surface, including the doors, as a canvas. You can find inspiration for making up your own designs or pictures almost anywhere.

Glazed doors

Glazed doors can be painted following the sequence recommended for panelled doors, starting with the area around each pane of glass. If the door is multi-paned or entirely glass except for the frame, treat it like a large casement window instead. Protect the panes from splashes with tape or a paint shield (see pages 20–21).

Protecting the floor

Use a paint shield or a piece of cardboard under the door frame to prevent the brush picking up dust from the floor and to protect the floor from paint. This is applicable when painting skirting boards too.

Protecting the floor

1 As well as keeping paint off the floor, card under a door or skirting board stops dust from spoiling the finish.

Further ideas for painting doors

▲ *Brilliantly coloured high-gloss paint has been used here: flame in the hallway area and bright Matisse-blue woodwork inside the room. With the door open, the effect is busy, vibrant and full of contrasts, but when the door is closed no blue will be visible from the landing.*

Two-colour doors

1 *Use two different colours, but make sure that none of the wrong colour is visible when the door is closed.*

Different colours on either side of a door

It often happens that a door needs to be painted in different colours on each side, corresponding to the decoration of the rooms or areas it links. It does not matter which side you paint first, but it is important that every part of the surface you see on one side of the door matches.

For the purpose of description, imagine the door opens from a passage into a room. On the opening side, paint the architrave, the frame up to and including the edge of the door stop, the leading edge of the door and the door face in one colour. On the other side, where the door faces the passage, in the second colour, paint the architrave and frame up to and over the doorstop, the hinged edge of the door and its other face.

Faux panel effect for flush doors

To lift the flatness of a flush door, painting *faux* panels creates an effective three-dimensional illusion. First measure up your door. Determine the number and size of the panels you want, and the dimensions of the *faux* rails and stiles. Measure and draw in the panels in pencil directly onto the surface. Mix up two shades of the chosen door colour, one lighter than the other, and then apply the darkest shade to each of the panels. When dry, paint the rest of the door in the lighter colour, beginning with the centre stiles, progressing to the rails, and finally paint the outer stiles. When completely dry, you can paint in the shading at the sides of the panels to give the panels depth. You will need a further darker version of the

Painting fake panels on a flush door

1 Measure and draw panels with a pencil before painting them in a slightly darker shade of your chosen colour.

2 When the panels have dried, paint what remains in a lighter shade, in the usual order (see pages 22–23).

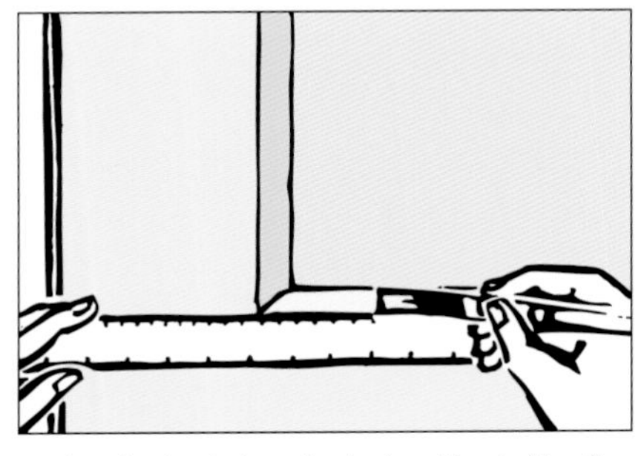

3 When the door is dry, paint the 'mouldings' with a fine brush, using a ruler; make sure the corners are mitred.

4 Taking note of the natural light source, use a lighter shade on two sides to reinforce the illusion.

◀ *Several* faux panels *have been incorporated here to create a simple, triumphant and humorous* trompe-l'oeil *door – complete with cat flap, letter box and bolts. The colours are strong and joyful, and the panels have been roughly outlined and left unshaded, proving that stylish interiors can also be witty.*

original colour and a paler version too. Establish in which direction your light source (real or imaginary) will hit the door. The tops of the panels and the sides closest to the light should be lined in the darker tone; the bottoms and further sides in the lighter tone. The thicker the lines you draw, the deeper your panel will appear to be. It is not advisable to make them too thick. You must judge this to suit the proportions of the panels you have created and choose the width of your brush accordingly. A fine brush is recommended. Use a wooden or plastic ruler with a bevelled top. Turn the bevel against the door so that it stands proud of the surface. Line the ruler up with the edge of the panel, rest the ferrule of the brush on the inside edge, and drag the brush gently along it. You will need to mitre each corner, so be sure to let the paint dry before attempting this in the corner where the two tones meet. If you do not feel you have a steady enough hand to use a ruler, you can create the lines by applying strips of low-tack masking tape and painting between these instead.

Finishes for woodwork

Doors and windows that are made of wood do not have to be painted to look good or complement a decorative scheme. They can be left bare, completely stripped of old paint, varnish or any other finish to allow the beauty of the grain to be admired. The two possible disadvantages of leaving wood unfinished are that it is not protected from dirt such as greasy fingermarks and that the stripping process may have left the wood dry and even slightly rough. The wood of old doors which have been industrially stripped in hot chemicals is likely to be in the worst condition; cold chemicals do not do nearly so much damage but are more expensive. Sanding will help and may even cure a roughened surface. In addition, there are a number of finishes that can enhance or seal bare wood to protect it from dirt. Before choosing a particular type of finish, do some research to make sure the finish will achieve the results you want.

Before applying any coloured finish, practise on a piece of wood of the same type until you get the right effect. Where more than one material needs to be applied in succession, use products from the same brand to avoid incompatibility and later problems. Always follow the manufacturer's instructions.

Staining

There are many different types of stain, all of which you wipe onto the woodwork with a wad of cloth, except for mouldings when, for greater accuracy, it is better to use a brush. Quick-drying stains can be tricky to apply evenly, so try out the colour first on a spare piece of wood. If staining a door, lie it flat before you start, so that the colour does not run. Wood must be clean and completely free of other finishes before application.

Water-based stains give the brightest and best colours. DIY shops tend to favour shades of brown, which reflect natural wood colours. Oil- and spirit-based stains are also available. Household dyes in many colours are widely available, and today, various types of coloured stains can be bought from specialist paint suppliers. Some sell pigments or concentrates with which you can mix up your own colour; some stains are concentrated and can be thinned to the shade you want, giving anything from an intense colour to a washed-out effect. You can also make your own stain by seriously watering down emulsion so that the grain will show through when it is brushed onto the wood. A stain does not give wood protection from wear, so consider adding a varnish or sealant; seal either the whole door or window, or only the areas around handles where fingers may eventually make dirty patches.

Varnishing

To protect bare or stained wood from becoming marked, you can paint it with a varnish or sealant. Varnish is available in a clear form, coloured in shades of brown or tinted with more interesting colours. Some types have three alternative finishes: gloss, silk and matt.

Oil-based varnish that is billed as 'clear' generally has a yellowish tinge that will become more yellow with age or in direct sunlight. Acrylic (water-based) varnish is clear and does not yellow with age. In steamy rooms, oil-based varnish is better. For extremely hard-wearing qualities, look for varnish containing Teflon. It should be noted that coloured varnishes are very difficult to remove, should you ever want a change.

Varnish is simply brushed on. For a really smooth finish, rub down with sandpaper between coats.

Oiling

Bare wood doors can be nourished and given a soft, mellow glow with specialist oil or even stale olive oil. All oils will darken the wood to some degree. Linseed oil mixed equally with button polish will give a slight sheen. Some finishing oils are waterproof. Rub oil into the bare wood using a soft cloth. Except for some special finishing oils, oil does not protect against dirt and spillages.

Waxing

Wax is not waterproof and may pick up grime unless the wood is first treated with a sealant. Colour can be added to clear wax such as beeswax by melting it gently with artist's oil colour. This should be allowed to

▲ *Varnish, whether clear or tinted, will allow the grain of the wood beneath to show through. Where the colour of the walls is bold, doors in good condition will often look their best left unpainted. Using wax, stain or varnish, as on this landing, the light wood of door, floor and ledge becomes a major, brightening and cohesive feature.*

cool before application. Alternatively, you could use a coloured shoe polish.

When polished up, wax gives a glossier finish than oil but, like oil, it allows the grain of the wood to show through. Wax does not protect against dirt and spillages.

Bleaching

Wood can be lightened to give a soft, sun-bleached effect, like that of driftwood. Use specialized wood bleach available from good decorator's suppliers.

Liming

Especially suitable for oak and other woods with a distinctive grain pattern, this milky finish lightens and adds interest to natural wood. Liming wax and liming kits are available from specialist paint and wood product suppliers. They come with clear instructions, but the process basically involves opening the grain of the wood by scrubbing along it with a wire brush, cleaning, working in the liming wax, wiping off the excess and polishing the dried wax. The wood must be clean and completely free of other finishes before application.

Staining the wood between cleaning and liming will make the liming more noticeable. You can also obtain a similar effect to liming by repeatedly painting bare wood with coats of watered-down white or lightly coloured emulsion then wiping it off. This finish will need sealing with varnish.

▶ *If you feel that the liming process, when carried out properly, sounds too long-winded, or too complicated, try the cheat's method: a similar effect can be achieved quite easily by painting bare wood with several coats of watered-down emulsion, wiping off the excess each time, and then sealing with a coat of varnish.*

Using paper, fabric and metal

In addition to the more conventional ways of painting or finishing doors described earlier (see pages 22–27), there are several exciting treatments which can be applied to them. With a little imagination and a bit of flair, any door can be transformed into a work of art by decorating it with painted patterns or large pictures.

Doors can also be covered with materials as diverse as different types of paper, fabric or even sheet metal.

Papering doors

If you do not feel up to devising an all-over design yourself, you can cover a flush door with virtually any kind of paper and varnish over it. The door and paper both need to be clean and the type of adhesive used should be appropriate for the job.

To create a bright and jolly, even kitsch, look, inexpensive paper items such as the covers of fashion or interiors magazines and brightly coloured packaging of food products – especially those from other parts of the world – can be used. The latter would be particularly appropriate in a kitchen.

For a more sophisticated look, you could use black and white or delicately coloured paper such as old sheet music, pages from out-of-date road atlases or maps, newspapers (which will yellow), old prints bought from a street market, photocopies of prints in a book or even old letters.

Textile cover-up

Another approach is to face the door with a single piece of fabric such as green baize, coloured felt or vinyl 'leather', using decorative brass-headed upholstery pins. Obviously the material needs to suit the overall decor of the room.

The material can be cut to the exact size of the door and glued on all over with an adhesive appropriate for the fabric. It must be smoothed out to ensure it is bubble-free and the edges must be turned back, if necessary, and securely glued down. Alternatively, the material can be slightly padded and secured with tacks. This gives a more generous, sophisticated look and is easier to remove when you want a change.

▲ *Metal foil has been applied to the surface of the door to provide an unusual and extremely eye-catching focal point in this silver-themed room. Applying metal foil to wood is a straightforward – if time-consuming – job, but the results are worth the effort. Finish with a layer of clear glaze to prevent damage to the foil's surface.*

▲ *Large, square, black metal studs appear at intervals around the raised parts of a pair of handsome panelled doors – and in the corners! Although the studs have been used sparingly, their effect is impressive and the overall look of the doors is reminiscent of a medieval castle. Heavy knobs provide the finishing touch.*

A padded door

First remove the door handle and then paint the edges of the door and a few centimetres around the edges of the front of the side you are covering. Choose a colour that tones in with the facing material. Cut a piece of wadding slightly smaller than the size of the door. This wadding could be a length of curtain interlining or a piece of leftover carpet underlay. Fix this to the door using tacks or a staple gun (available from hardware stores to suit various sizes of staple).

Before attaching the facing material over the wadding, mark the door at regular intervals around the edge where the tacks are to go. Cut the fabric slightly larger than the door. Turn back the edges so that you have a panel of fabric the same size as the door. Press these edges, if appropriate for the fabric, and then glue or sew them down. At the same time, cut off the bulk of the material at the corners and fold back, first along one edge and then the other, to mitre them.

Decorative tacks for attaching this fabric panel can be bought from suppliers of upholstery equipment in a variety of designs and sizes, including the traditional brass-coloured domed-top type. Alternatively, simply attach the fabric to the door with a staple gun, then hide the staples by gluing a braid or edging over them.

Attach the fabric to the door, making sure the material is hanging straight. Fix a tack (or staple) through the centre top of the material into the middle of the top of the door. Make sure that the tension is just right – not too tight and not slack – and position the second tack through the centre of the bottom of the material into the middle of the bottom of the door.

Finish attaching the fabric along the top, bottom and lastly the sides, always checking tension and (using the weave if there is one) that it is straight. Place a tack in each corner for a neat finish. Other tacks can be placed on the door face in lines to make a pattern or a panel effect.

Cut a small hole through the layers of fabric for the spindle of the door handle or door knob. Fix the door handle or knob back in place.

Sheet metal

For a really dramatic, industrial-style finish, face a door with sheet metal such as zinc or stainless steel. This is not a difficult job, but requires care, and the end result can be stunning. Begin by measuring the door precisely. Then find a steel stockholder who will supply you with a single panel of metal and cut it to size. From the wide choice available, choose a metal and finish you like, bearing in mind that a lightweight flush door may only be able to support a thin sheet of metal. The optimum thickness is 1mm (1/16in).

When the piece is to be cut, specify that the corners must be cut exactly square, and the sheet must be without scratches or blemishes. Handle pieces with extreme care as the burred edges can cut, and smooth the edges with heavy-duty wet-and-dry paper.

You can attach the metal to the door using a wide range of finishes and sizes of fixing, including escutcheon pins, drive pins, roundhead screws, pop rivets and even tin tacks. The choice of fixing is entirely personal, as the finishes are equally effective. Pop rivets give a particularly pleasing industrial look and are applied with a pop riveter, which is available from hardware and DIY stores.

Whichever fixing you select, begin by drilling a small hole through the metal and into the wood, using a drill bit of the same diameter as your fixing or slightly smaller (experiment on a scrap of wood). If you are hanging a new door, you can attach the metal before hanging it, to make working along the bottom edge easier. Otherwise, attach the metal at the top first so it hangs down while you fix the rest. Use an adhesive suitable for gluing metal to wood, or double-sided tape, to ensure that the edges of the metal sheet stick properly to the door. Attach the metal with fixings applied in any pattern you choose, perhaps by using a combination of sizes or types for a more elaborate effect.

To make a hole for the door-knob fitting, first drill a small hole in the metal, to act as a guide, then a larger hole with a 1.5cm (1/2in) drill bit. If you are in any doubt about your ability to do this correctly, there is always the option of getting a professional to fit it for you.

Metal sheeting and rivets can of course be used to transform the doors of cupboards anywhere in the house, but it is not necessary to use real metal to create the look. Metallic paint is effective too. Car paints are available from car goods suppliers in a range of colours as well as the silvery grey associated with real aluminium or steel.

◀ *These impressive doors have been covered on one side with rich red leather, a stunning treatment that is further enhanced by rows of brass studs arranged to imitate panelling. Upholstery tacks could be used to similar effect.*

Making a padded door

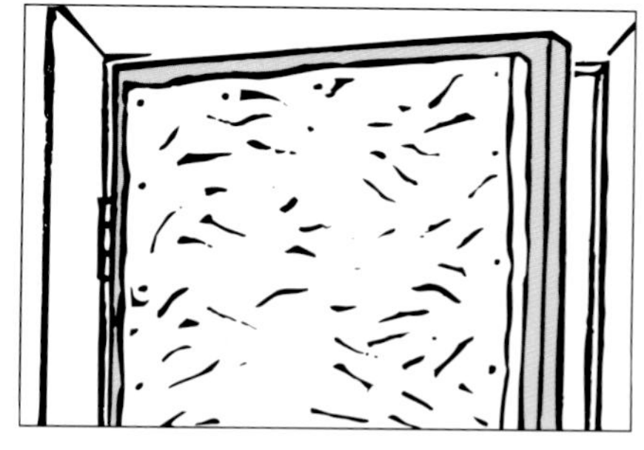

1 *Cut a piece of wadding slightly smaller than the size of the door, and attach its edges with a staple gun or tacks.*

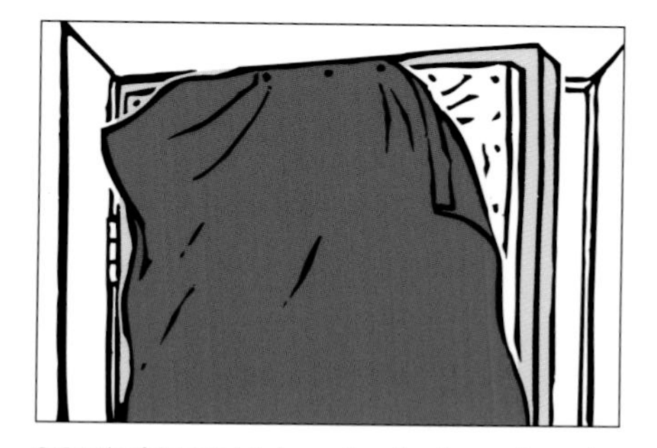

2 *Cut the fabric slightly larger than the door and turn the edges over. Start fixing at the centre top of the door.*

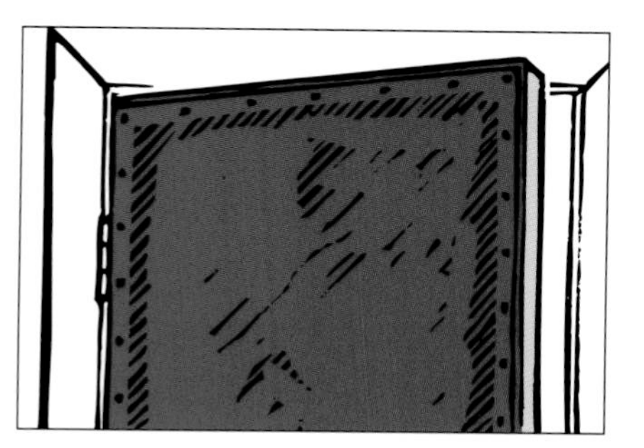

3 *Finish attaching the fabric at the top, then the bottom, followed by the sides, using fixings at regular intervals.*

Effects for glass

▶ *Preserving privacy and yet allowing natural light to filter in, different types of glass combine happily around two sides of this walk-in shower: glass blocks divide it from the bath, while the door has been etched. A similar effect to this chequerboard with palm trees can be achieved using a frosting technique.*

Frosted, patterned and coloured glass have long been used for window panes to give privacy or simply to add a decorative aspect to a window. Coloured glass has been popular for centuries and since the early nineteenth century homes have been decorated with coloured, cut, etched and painted panes. Coloured glass can be used to make windows and glazed doors more interesting and it becomes really beautiful when sunlight streams through it, creating pools of tinted light on walls and ceilings. Frosted windows are useful where light needs to be admitted to a room where an element of screening is also required.

Frosted glass

Interior designers use a wonderful cheat, without embarrassment, to create a patterned frosted window – frosted-effect self-adhesive plastic. It is available in a variety of weights and finishes from sign-writing, specialist decorating shops and even hardware stores. The plastic can be used in sheets to cover a whole pane of glass or cut out to create individual designs. When creating a design this way, you will need to take into account to which side of the glass you will fix the plastic. In a bathroom, where condensation may get between the glass and the plastic, it may be preferable to apply the design to the outer side of the door. If this is the case, make sure that your original design has the image in reverse.

For a different frosted effect, self-adhesive plastic (not necessarily frosted) can be used as a mask, and around it a mixture of white paint and varnish can be stippled. Begin by drawing your design on paper (bear in mind that the shapes you cut out from it will represent the unfrosted part of the final window). Use a fine black marker. You could pin the paper to the window and draw *in situ*. Where

Frosted glass

1 Lay the design underneath sticky-backed plastic, transfer the design and cut it out with a craft knife.

2 Once the design has been cut, peel the sticky plastic off the backing and stick the shapes onto the window pane.

3 Stipple the paint solution onto the surface of the glass, overlapping it onto the edges of the plastic shapes.

4 When the paint is dry, peel the plastic shapes away from the window to reveal the clear glass underneath.

there are two or more windows beside each other, the design could be made to flow across them in one unified image.

Tape the finished drawing to a hard horizontal surface. Tape the self-adhesive plastic over the design, trace through it and cut out the shapes from the plastic with a craft knife. To transfer a complicated design to the window, it may be worth taking care to cut through the plastic only, not the backing, in order to keep the pieces together. Alternatively, tape the design to the back of the window and align the cut-out plastic pieces on the other front. Either way, the glass must be scrupulously clean and dry. Peel the plastic design(s) off the backing sheet and rub down onto the glass, being careful not to catch or lift the edges.

Mix up equal quantities of white gloss oil paint and matt polyurethane varnish (you will not need a great deal: three tablespoons of each will be enough for quite a large window). Having fixed the design to the window, apply the paste, using a stencilling brush, with a light stippling action. Leave until completely dry before removing the plastic from the window. A craft knife will be needed to lift the corners of the plastic. Finally protect the pattern using a spray acrylic aerosol varnish, which will coat the design effectively.

Painted glass

You can install a window or panel of real stained glass that has been specially designed and made for you by a craftsman, but a much cheaper alternative is to paint a glass panel in imitation of a stained-glass window. You can obtain special glass paints for this and fake lead strips or special relief paste for separating the colours from art shops, but you can also use artist's oil colours, thinned to a greater or lesser extent with linseed oil and turpentine or white spirit and mixed with a small amount of polyurethane varnish.

Draw your design first on paper. It need not imitate traditional stained glass found in churches and Victorian houses. Look at contemporary art and abstract stained glass for inspiration. It may be wise, on a first attempt, to keep to simple geometric shapes.

The best method for achieving this is to paint a piece of glass, keeping it flat to avoid colours running, and replace the existing glass in a window with this new piece. However, it is possible to paint on glass *in situ*, provided the paint is kept sufficiently viscous. The glass must be completely clean, free from grease (including fingermarks) and dry.

Lay the design behind the glass and secure it in place with masking tape. Use special relief paste to demarcate the outlines of the design, using your drawing beneath as a guide. Fill in the areas with paint using a fine artist's brush. Take care to avoid the paint running by ensuring there is minimal paint loaded on your brush. Thin layers can be built up if necessary. If you make mistakes, either remove the paint while wet with a clean rag dipped in white spirit or scrape it off when dry. When the design is completed, allow the paints to dry thoroughly before spraying with polyurethane varnish.

◀ *The panels of this kitchen door have been painted red and yellow to create an idiosyncratic look that adds the finishing touch to this personalized, madcap kitchen. An effect like this is easy to achieve with glass paints, and can be done either before or after the panels have been put in place. Even small areas treated in this way will enliven a space instantly.*

Painted glass

1 *Tape the design behind the glass, trace out the design on the glass with leading paste and leave it to dry.*

2 *Using an artist's brush, fill in the areas between the leading paste with specialist paints formulated for glass.*

Cleaning up and problems with paintwork

Tools and equipment should be cleaned and put away before the finish dries on them. Close a can by placing a piece of wood across the top of the lid and tapping it with a hammer. Throw away dirty rags in an outside dustbin, preferably a metal one, after chemicals have evaporated. Clean metal tools such as shavehooks with water or white spirit and put them away.

▲ *Gloss paint can look stunning. Here, panelled walls and a wooden door have been given a glossy sheen with a warm shade of cream which reflects the incoming sunlight. However, if undercoat or primer is incorrectly applied, a top coat of gloss can end up looking dull. If this happens, wait for the paint to dry, sand and clean it, then re-apply the gloss.*

Cleaning and storing brushes

If you take the time to care correctly for your brushes, you will greatly extend their life. Wash brushes used for water-based paint or wood stains in water. For brushes used for oil painting, wash in white spirit to loosen the paint then wash in warm soapy water; proprietary brush cleaner is expensive but worthwhile if you have invested in the best brushes. Rinse cleaned brushes thoroughly, then work them against a clean rag to get the worst of the water off.

For overnight storage, suspend brushes with oil-based paint on them in water, with the brushes clear of the bottom, by a wire through a drilled hole in the handle. For shorter-term storage, wrap in foil or clingfilm to keep them wet.

For long-term storage, when brushes are clean, shake any excess water off the brush and place a rubber band around the bristles to help it to keep its shape as it dries. Rest it on its side. When completely dry, wrap brushes in paper and store in a dry place.

Cleaning up paint spills and splashes

Paint on glass is quite easy to remove. Let it dry and then scrape it off. Dry paint on the floor is more difficult. On wood, scrape it off carefully as for glass, taking care not to scratch the surface. It may be necessary to sand a paint blob very carefully, trying not to damage the surrounding wood and, if necessary, touching up the floor with scratch cover or other wood treatment.

Paint on a carpet is extremely difficult to remove. If the paint is only lightly on the surface of a carpet with a pile, it may be possible to snip away the top of fibres when the paint is dry. If it has soaked into the carpet, you can try removing it with a strong dry-cleaning fluid, but this may spread the colour. If the stain cannot be removed, it will be necessary to cut out and replace a small square of carpet.

If you get paint on a recently painted wood surface, lightly sand the surface and touch up with the appropriate colour. In certain situations, if a blob of oil paint has splashed onto a water-based paint for example, it may be necessary to prime the patch before repainting.

Paint problems

Blistering

This will occur if moisture has been trapped between the layers of paint. To correct, strip off the offending layers (this is not difficult if the blistering is extensive, as much of it will simply peel off) and re-apply the paint. Blistering may also occur if the wrong type of paint has been applied – for example, a water-based paint over a layer of oil-based paint – so check that your paints are compatible.

Wrinkling or sagging

If you apply paint too heavily, it will begin to sag. To resolve this, wait until the paint is dry, sand sufficiently heavily for a smooth surface and re-apply the top coat. Alternatively, strip off all the top coats entirely and re-apply the paint less heavily.

Dribbles

This is a consequence of too much paint on the brush. If you notice a dribble or 'run' as you are painting, work across it with your brush before the final laying off (see pages 18–19). If the dribble has begun to dry, leave it until it is completely dry, then sand it down and touch up as necessary.

Undercoat showing through

This could happen for a number of reasons. Either the wrong colour undercoat has been used (too dark for a pale top coat or too pale for a dark top coat) or the top coat has been applied too sparingly. You may even have forgotten to add a second top coat. To rectify, paint on another layer or two of top.

Storing brushes used for oil painting

1 *For long-term storage, wash brushes first in white spirit to loosen the paint, then in warm soapy water.*

2 *For overnight storage, suspend unwashed brushes in jam jars filled with water, or wrap in paper or clingfilm.*

▲ *A beautifully smooth paint finish in vivid yellow draws the eye towards this window frame and the garden beyond. Few of us have so steady a hand that we can paint a window frame without leaving splashes on the panes. Fortunately, paint is easily removed from glass; simply wait for the paint to dry, then carefully scrape it off.*

Foreign bodies stuck in the paint

Wet paint will trap anything that touches it, such as clothing fibres, dust specks or small insects. Experts usually recommend leaving the paint until it is dry, then sanding and touching up with paint. But if the paint is wet and the foreign body is just one item (a fly or paintbrush bristle, for example, rather than a cloud of dust) you might feel confident enough to have a go at removing it in one neat swipe with a clean rag.

Crazing

This will appear if one layer of paint has been applied before a previous one was completely dry, or if the paints are not compatible. Unfortunately the only way to correct crazing is to strip off the paint completely and re-apply.

Paint will not dry

This occurs for several reasons. Either the paint was not stirred properly before application, the surface was not clean, or the weather is too hot and humid. Try opening the windows for a few days, if possible. If this does not work, you will have to strip off the paint and re-apply, this time making sure the surface is absolutely clean.

Gloss looks dull

This is caused if the primer and/or undercoat was improperly applied (or omitted) or is not completely dry. Alternatively, the top coat could have been applied during frosty or exceptionally cold weather. You will have to wait for the paint to dry completely, then sand lightly, clean the surface thoroughly and apply another top coat during normal weather conditions.

Brush marks show

This will occur if cheap brushes, which are more likely to leave brush marks in paintwork than better-quality ones, were used and/or the paint was applied too thickly and not laid off properly (see pages 18–19). To address this problem, sand, wash and dry thoroughly, then re-apply the top coat using a good-quality brush, and taking special care with your technique.

Directory of window and door furniture

Doors and windows are equipped with various fittings to facilitate their movement and security. Generally referred to as 'furniture', these fittings may be unobtrusive or more decorative and in a style to suit the period of your home. Except for some door knobs and handles, they are usually made of metal, including iron, brass and chrome.

Additional paraphernalia can be fitted to doors to perform various functions, including providing security with bolts and locks. A front door might also be fitted with a spy hole, a knocker, a letter plate and house numbers, with a bell nearby on the outside wall. These items can be handsome or elaborate antiques, reproductions or interesting modern designs, or anything in between so long as they are appropriate to the door in scale and design.

Doors

Knobs

Door knobs are twisted to operate the opening mechanism, except for those on cupboards which are designed to be pulled. Traditionally, they are made of iron, brass, glass, china, plastic or wood, and are sometimes finished in other materials like copper or chrome. Some eighteenth- and nineteenth-century examples are elaborately decorated and mounted on interestingly shaped back plates. Contemporary designs range in shape and type from sleek steel to coloured resin 'shells'. Old knobs can be bought from industrial stripping workshops, second-hand markets and junk or antique shops. 1

Handles

Because of the pressure exerted on them, handles are usually made in fairly robust materials such as iron, brass or plastic. Their design ranges widely.

Rim latches and locks

A rim latch contains the opening mechanism of a door in a metal box which is fitted to the door's surface. The box may be plain and painted black (as are most modern ones) or it may be more decorative. Brass rim latches and locks are available in imitation of antique ones that were fitted to the doors of important rooms in the eighteenth and nineteenth centuries. Rim latches have an appealingly unpretentious appearance especially suited to old houses and cottages but do not seem to have caught the imagination of contemporary door furniture designers in the way that knobs and handles have.

Because they can be prised or kicked off a door, rim latches are less secure than mortise latches (below) and therefore not generally acceptable for exterior doors. 3

Mortise latches and locks

A mortise latch or lock is fitted into the thickness of the door and is thus hidden from view. Insurance companies generally specify the type of mortise lock acceptable to them for exterior door security. 2

Thumb latches

A thumb latch is the type of fastening mechanism that is appropriate on battened cottage-type doors. You grip a vertical handle while pressing down on a protruding iron (or wood, if the latch is wooden) plate just above it. This raises the sneck which lifts the bolt (known as the 'beam') to open or secure the door. All the mechanics of the fastening are on the surface of the door, which gives the thumb latch a special charm and interest.

Escutcheons

These are the small plates, sometimes with a swinging flap for draught exclusion, which surround keyholes. Door handle back plates often incorporate an escutcheon.

Finger plates

These are narrow rectangular panels placed vertically above and sometimes below a door knob. They are designed to protect much-used doors from greasy fingermarks. Antique ones are made of the same variety of non-porous materials as door knobs; modern ones are just as likely to be made of plastic, resin or a metal such

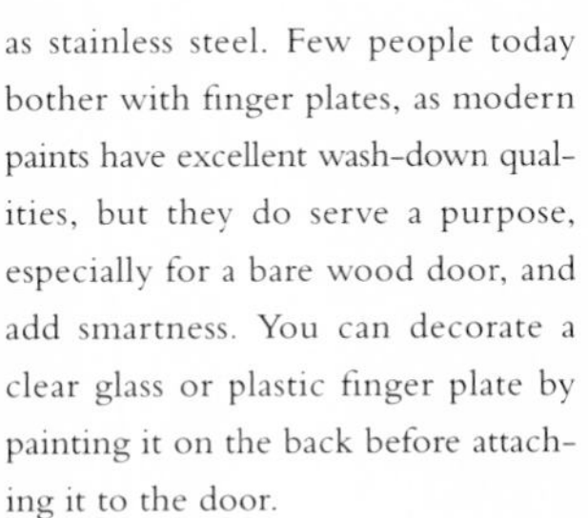

as stainless steel. Few people today bother with finger plates, as modern paints have excellent wash-down qualities, but they do serve a purpose, especially for a bare wood door, and add smartness. You can decorate a clear glass or plastic finger plate by painting it on the back before attaching it to the door.

Hinges

Hinges are barely noticeable, except for the elongated type used on battened cottage doors. Often shaped and decorative, these are usually painted black, in contrast to the colour of the door. The recessed hinges used on a

4

5

panelled or flush door are usually either brass, in which case they should not be painted, or iron, which can be painted. It is advisable to remove paint from the screw heads so that they can be unscrewed easily at a later date if necessary. 4

Portière

This is an ingenious fitting which aids draught exclusion around a doorway. Consisting of a hinged metal curtain pole attached to the wall at one end and the door at the other, it hangs a curtain across the inside of the door and opens with it.

Windows

Sash fasteners

These secure the two parts of a sash window, pushing them apart vertically and together horizontally. By pushing the sashes firmly into the frame, the action also cuts out draughts. Sash stays come in a variety of designs, most commonly traditional styles made either from iron, which you oil or paint, or lacquered brass, which you do not.

Casement fasteners

Casements require two fittings, a fastener at the side and a stay along the bottom which not only helps to keep the window closed but also allows it to be left open without flapping. Perhaps the prettiest design widely available is the rat-tail, which ends in a spiral shape.

Metal casements often have a cockspur fastener, where the part that turns onto the window has two or more teeth, allowing the window to be fastened open just a fraction for ventilation.

Espagnolette

This is the long bolt that fastens a pair of French windows. A handle, fitted on one of the windows, turns the bolt, which shoots up and down into the window frame. 5

Restoring metal fittings

Door and window furniture can be cleaned then restored with household metal polish, paint stripper or old-fashioned recipes.

First wash the item thoroughly with soap and water or a solution of soda crystals, to enable you to establish its condition. Then clean it up: old lacquer can be removed with acetone; soak iron fittings in paraffin before scrubbing with wire wool to remove rust; wash chrome with a solution of washing-up liquid and a small dash of ammonia; de-tarnish brass by rubbing it with a half-lemon sprinkled with salt. Finally, polish the item with a product appropriate to the material in which it is finished. If you like a bright finish and do not like polishing, add clear acrylic lacquer.

Curtains

Besides their obvious practical merits of draught exclusion and the creation of privacy, curtains are popular in homes because they create an aura of comfort and a pleasing atmosphere. As soon as curtains are hung up at the window of a bare room, they make it look like a home. Furthermore, they can be used to create almost any effect, depending on the type of fabric and how it is used: sheer floaty curtains are romantic; enormous padded ones are grand and pretty; checked ones are fresh and cottagey.

When deciding upon the type of curtains for a room, it is important to bear in mind the overall decorative scheme. Its design and the colours used in it will reflect your personal style and preferences.

Considering the options

There are many factors to take into consideration. Look at the room carefully. Study the size, shape and position of the window or windows and take into account the period and proportions of both the window and the room. In a period house, curtains can reflect the style of that period or not, as you choose, but they tend to look better if they are in sympathy with the architectural proportions of the room. Small curtains that only just cover a window will look silly in a Georgian or Victorian room with a high ceiling, for instance, as will a neat cottage casement puffed up with an over-sized, over-grand window treatment.

It is possible to have more than one style of window treatment in a single room, creating more visual interest and giving the opportunity of using a more extravagant or expensive fabric than you might otherwise consider. For example, where there are three windows in a row, the middle one could have generous, billowing, floor-length curtains while those to each side could be fitted with a handsome Roman blind (see pages 68–73) made of the same fabric. This would create a sophisticated and dramatic effect using about the same amount of fabric as skimpy curtains for all three windows.

A window does not necessarily have to have two curtains. One may be enough if a window is hard up against a wall on one side or if several windows are close together. In the latter case an extra curtain at the other end of the row will balance appearances when they are drawn back during the day.

Light and warmth

Another important consideration to bear in mind is the direction the room faces and how light and warm it is as a result. Where there is plenty of direct sunlight, a single, large curtain could be fixed across the top of each window, for example, and pulled back to one side during the day. On the other hand, if the room is dark and faces away from the sun, the amount of light available can be maximized with curtains that pull back completely clear of the window. Lining the rebate with mirror will reflect more light into the room and can make narrow windows appear wider. To warm a room, soft sheer curtains can be used to filter cold light, while heavy, flanking over-curtains create a cosy effect.

◀ This window is framed with layers of fabric in the same colours – terracotta and cream – but in different patterns: the Roman blind in a simple check is edged with the same tasselled braid as a cushion, while heavy interlined curtains are made from bold stripes edged with green.

◀◀ The ultimate no-sew curtain, this diaphanous fabric floating in the breeze has been cut to double the length required and hung over a slender pole outside the door, to filter bright sunlight. White, rough-plastered walls and blue-painted woodwork on the doors and windows contribute to the seaside look.

Curtain lengths

Naturally, curtains can be any size you choose, but most often are one of three lengths: sill, below sill or floor.

Floor length

Floor-length curtains either just skim the floor or billow onto it. They look generous, generally make a stronger visual statement than short curtains and, at their most magnificent, can be stunning. They will show off a beautiful or large-patterned fabric to best effect and they will balance a handsome pelmet, beneath which short curtains would look silly. They make sense for a window that is taller than it is wide, especially if it is exceptionally tall and narrow or if it comes down to the floor. They may also be more appropriate to the period of your house, if for instance it is Victorian with sash windows or even Georgian. Floor-length curtains

▲ *A length of muslin, tie-dyed in vibrant colours and knotted at each end, is looped over a simple wooden pole. This sill-length curtain is dramatic and will veil a dull view, but won't give draught exclusion or much privacy. The window's exuberant cut-out frame adds to its impact.*

are also best for draught exclusion, especially if they drape luxuriously on the floor.

Long curtains use the most fabric and are therefore more expensive to make than shorter ones, but you do get more curtain for your effort. Another factor in their favour is that, if you are a beginner and worried about getting your hems straight, even a couple of centimetres out will not show with curtains that drape on the floor.

Sill length

Short curtains look more cottagey than long ones and suit small windows as well as those that are square or wider than they are tall. They either fall a little below the sill or just to it but not quite touching it; a prominent sill, or a window seat, will certainly dictate the latter, as anything longer will not fall straight. Below-sill-length curtains are more effective at keeping out draughts, as the entire window, including the sill, is completely hidden. They also look more generous than curtains that only just touch the sill.

Shorter curtains which barely graze the sill are practical in a kitchen or bathroom, although a blind would perhaps be a better and more economical choice.

Budgeting

Whatever your style preference, your budget is also a significant factor. It will influence your choice of fabric, which varies widely in cost, as well as the amount of material you can afford to buy. Even on a limited budget, however, extra-long, extra-full curtains are not out of the question, for they can be made of inexpensive fabric and can be left unlined. Alternatively, consider other styles of curtain and combinations with blinds (see pages 66–77) which can achieve a similar effect using much less fabric, such as pull-up curtains (see pages 74–75) or a blind beneath a pelmet.

▲ *An ingenious curtain made from pieces of Chinese paper, each decorated with a sheet of gold leaf and glued to a string of natural hemp pulled down with a weight. The paper is hung in carefully staggered rows so that the pieces do not touch and the light between them makes a zigzag pattern.*

Cost is an important factor when deciding whether to buy the curtains ready-made or to make them up yourself. A halfway measure would be to buy the fabric at a cost that suits you then ask someone else to make the curtains up for you. Other options for keeping costs low are to exercise patience and wait for the sales before buying fabric or ready-made curtains; to visit mill shops and buy direct; to buy, and perhaps re-make, second-hand curtains; or just to modify your initial idea for an elaborate curtain design into something more manageable.

Making up curtains

Making the curtains yourself (see pages 48–53) will obviously save money, but the design needs to be something that accords with your level of sewing experience and the time available. A limited budget can be a blessing, helping you to choose a simple and uncluttered contemporary style that will last. The more frilly and full the curtain, the more complicated it will be to make, the longer it will take and the more fabric it will require.

Suspension

The type of curtain hanging needs to be determined in context, considering all the details of the setting. You must decide whether you want the curtain to hang from rings on a pole or from a track (see pages 40–41), whether this will be left exposed, hidden by a pelmet (see pages 62–63) or set into a *faux* pole. If there is little space between ceiling and window, a pelmet is inadvisable as it will either look thin and mean or crouch down on the window; a pole is preferable in such a situation. If, on the other hand, there is plenty of space, and you want the window to appear taller than it is, a well-proportioned pelmet can help create an illusion of greater height.

Fabric

The choice of fabric suitable for making up into curtains is so huge it can seem baffling (see pages 44–47). Take the overall style of the room as your starting point and first establish which type of window decoration is most appropriate: flimsy fabric for creating floaty effects or for layering; plain fabric, pale or richly coloured, perhaps with a velvety pile or an interesting weave; refreshing checks or stripes; printed graphic motifs; traditional fabric like floral chintz, tartan, printed linen or *toile de Jouy*; picture fabric; ethnic-style fabric like crewelwork, kilim print or Indian hand-blocked cotton; rich silk or damask.

Practical considerations are often involved in the choice of a fabric. Silk, for example, fades and rots in sunlight and washable cotton is useful in a kitchen or bathroom. Scale is another factor: a large window can take a huge print that will look entirely out of proportion on a small window; and conversely a small print will look fiddly on a large window.

Trimming

Trimmings can make all the difference to curtains but they must be used with great care (see page 47). A constrasting braid or ribbon set back from the edge of a plain curtain or blind gives it weight and definition. A substantial fringe along the bottom of a pull-up curtain or Austrian blind can transform it, making it look serious and luxurious.

Lining

The final but important consideration is whether or not to have a lining (see pages 56–61). Lightweight, unlined curtains are the simplest to make, while lined curtains keep out light and draughts better and look more substantial. Curtains can be lined in two main ways. Heavy interlining is like solid padding between the front and lining fabrics; locked-in lining means the curtain lining is invisibly attached at intervals to the front fabric. Professional curtain makers say these hang better than loose-lined curtains, which are the simplest to make (see pages 58–59). Detachable linings are versatile as they can be taken off for laundering, or removed in summer to give the curtains a lighter effect.

◀ *Draping elegantly on the floor, these unlined curtains have an integral valance and are tied to a slender wooden pole. Because the curtains are made from pre-shrunk calico, and the valances, edging and ties from pre-shrunk linen union, they can easily be machine-washed.*

Directory of poles, tracks and accessories

Poles

Curtain poles are intended to be seen and to make a strong visual contribution to the overall look of a window and its dressing. They are altogether bolder and more demonstrative than curtain track, which is designed to be discreet and often hidden behind a pelmet or valance. Made in either wood or metal, there is a huge range of poles to choose from.

Poles are made in various diameters and are sold by length to suit your requirements. Pole kits, with brackets and rings included, are widely available. The poles come in set lengths and can be cut if required.

1

2

Wooden poles

Wooden poles are often finished at either end with a finial. Both poles and their rings (where these exist) can be painted, stained, oiled or waxed.

Natural wood suits many interiors. Plain black, grey or white looks discreet, or you could paint the pole to match the walls, the woodwork or the curtain fabric. For something as grand as richly coloured brocade, a gold-painted pole would be dramatic. Wooden poles without rings can be used with handmade cased or looped headings, for example. **1**

Lightweight rods

A variety of rods can be used to carry lightweight curtains and sheers, including wooden dowelling, plastic net rod and brass café rod. These slender rods are well suited to small windows and look good with cased, slotted and other headings that do not have rings. They take up little space and are therefore useful where the top of a window is just below a low ceiling. Light rods with a bracket and hinge at one end can be used in a dormer or other deep-set window; instead of drawing back the curtains the rods swing open during the day.

Metal poles

Metal poles and any rings are generally made of brass, iron or steel. Steel and iron poles, often painted black, could be painted any colour. **3**

Faux poles

Although a *faux* pole, or corded pole, is made to resemble a brass or wooden pole, it is not really a pole at all. It has track set into it, with rings masking the runners. A hidden pulley system opens and closes the curtains, which helps protect the fabric. An overlap arm can be used with *faux* poles.

Tracks

Curtain track consists of a rail and sliding runners into which the curtain hooks slot. Made of either plastic or metal, it is available in a huge variety of subtly different types and weights. Some are fitted with a corded pulley system which helps protect fine or delicate fabric from wear and tear. Some have an integral valance rail.

As track takes up little space, it is particularly useful in situations where there is almost no wall space between the top of a window and a low ceiling. It can be bent to fit around curves such as bay windows. When the curtains are pulled back, however, track will show unless it is hidden by a pelmet or other covering.

The length of track required is governed by the bulk of the curtains and the extent to which you want them to draw back from the window during the day. You can buy track in kits or you can buy all the parts separately according to your needs. The sliding runners are sold separately. **4**

4

Metal track

Stronger and longer-lasting than plastic, metal track is probably a better choice for heavy curtains, the weight of which may pull plastic track from the wall. If fitted with a corded pulley system, metal track provides the easiest way of drawing curtains around bends; in such cases it is best fitted professionally to ensure accurate results. Track can incorporate an overlap arm to allow one curtain to overlap the other when closed. Metal track can be painted with enamel paint.

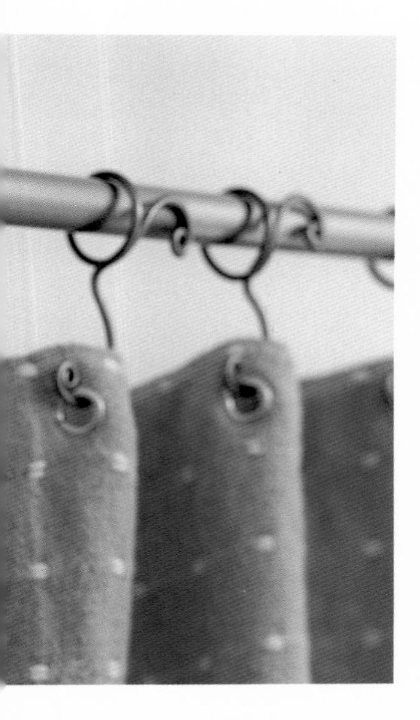

3

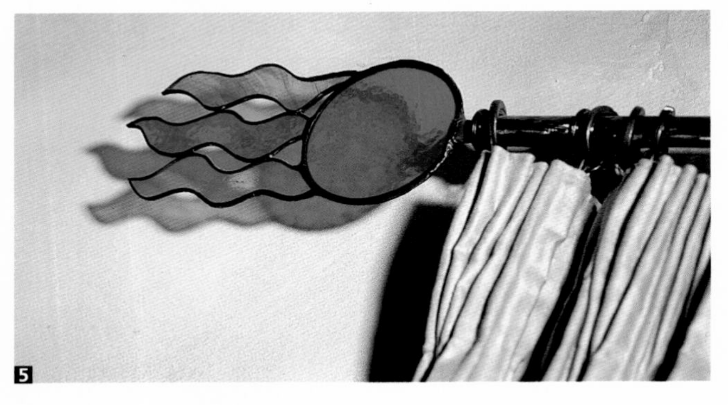

5

Plastic track

Plastic track is easier to fit than metal and adequate for light- to middle-weight curtains. It is easily bent around gentle corners, the ideal type for this being that with a metal core, as this keeps its shape better than track that is made entirely of plastic. Plastic track cannot be painted successfully.

Accessories

Rings

These are used with a curtain pole. If you buy a pole kit, the brackets and rings will be provided; otherwise, buy as many rings as you want separately, checking that they fit the pole, but not too tightly or they will be difficult to draw across. Allow for a ring at each end of the pole, between the bracket and the finial, to secure the outer edge of each curtain. 2

Curtain clips

These small curtain rings, with a decorative clip at the bottom instead of a hole for a hook, are most suitable for lightweight curtains. Before the clips are attached to the curtain fabric, the top edge of the fabric needs to be turned over twice and hemmed, with the raw edge of the lining, if any, sewn in under the hem. Clips should be attached to the top of the curtain at intervals, with one at each end.

Sewn-on rings

Sew small brass, metal or plastic rings to the curtain top at intervals, with one at each end. These are not suitable for heavy curtains, where the rings might pull and tear the fabric.

Hooks

In addition to standard plastic and metal curtain hooks which slot into heading tape and then into the runners or rungs, there are several clever types with special uses. Among these are the combined hook and slider, and the combined valance hook and glider. With the latter, the valance is divided and draws back with the curtain during the day, rather than remaining across the whole window like a pelmet.

Finials

A decorative finial is usually fitted onto each end of a pole. They finish the pole with a flourish and need to be in proportion to the pole. A fiddly little finial on the end of a stout pole, for instance, will look silly. There is a wide choice of finials, including balls, spear heads, arrow ends, curlicues, rams' heads, pineapples and many more, in a range of materials and finishes. 5

Cording sets

A cording set is useful if the curtains are especially fragile or fine as it removes the necessity of pulling on the curtains to draw them closed. Sets can be bought with track or separately. Electric curtain track is also available. This has a small motor at the end of the track which draws the curtains, activated either at the touch of a button or by a remote control unit.

Draw rods are a simple alternative to a cording set. These are plastic rods, one attached to the leading edge of each curtain, which allow curtains to be drawn manually but without the fabric being handled.

Valance track

This can be bought with track, or separately and added on later to most types of curtain track with the help of brackets and extension arms. Plastic valance track is easy to bend to shape.

Weights

These can be sewn into the hem of a curtain to give it added weight and help it hang well. They come in two forms: buttons and tape. Buttons are round weights with holes in the middle for sewing in place. If it is not sewn in position, a button weight will, in time, gradually move along the bottom of the curtain. Leadweight tape consists of a narrow tube of fabric containing small cylindrical weights which is placed in a continuous line along the bottom of the curtain hem.

Cord tidy

This small plastic shape solves the problem of what to do with the strings of a heading tape after the curtain has been gathered up. The strings are simply wound around the cord tidy, which is then tucked into one of the pockets in the tape. The strings should never be cut off; if they are, the curtain heading cannot be pulled flat for cleaning or alterations.

Fixing poles and tracks

Fixing poles

Poles are designed to be face-fixed to a wall with support brackets, one at each end and possibly an additional central bracket. Some poles can be end-fixed by slotting them into side wall fixings.

A bracket prevents the rings moving any further along the pole, so the position of the end brackets (and indeed the length of the pole) depends on the fullness of the curtain and how far back from the window you want the curtain to pull. A frequent mistake is to place the brackets too close to the window. As a guide, fix brackets at least 15cm (6in) out from the window frame on each side, and allow about 10cm (4in) between the bracket and the finial. The outer curtain ring sits between the bracket and the finial to hold the curtain in place when drawn.

The pole should be installed parallel with the top of the window, unless this is wildly out of true with the line of the ceiling, in which case you can position the pole either strictly level, using a spirit level, or somewhere in between level and parallel with the window, whichever looks better. The pole should be high enough above the window for the curtain to cut out light at the top, but not so high that there is a great expanse of wall between it and the top of the window.

If you would like the curtain to fall further into the room than the brackets allow – perhaps to clear a deep window sill or to fall in front of a blind – mount each bracket on a wooden block. The blocks can be finished in the same way as the wall, with paint or paper. As the brackets (or brackets and blocks) will be bearing considerable weight, ensure that they are securely fixed to the wall with long screws.

Fitting lightweight rods is easy as the ends can be slotted into small metal brackets with integral sockets, either recessed or face-fixed. Telescopic rods are also available; they have an internal spring that enables them to expand to fit the window. Dowelling, being less rigid than a proper curtain pole, needs to be well supported in the middle to prevent it sagging. A small decorative hook of the type onto which you loop a tie-back will do the job. Generally speaking, the thicker the

▲ *Simple cotton curtains are hung with iron rings sewn directly to the top of the curtain. The rings are then strung on a narrow iron pole with decorative curled finials. Because the pole is narrow and the curtains long and therefore quite heavy, the pole is given added support by a central bracket.*

▶ *Pretty gingham curtains are ideal for the kitchen of a country house. They are hung from a standard curtain track which is concealed by a covered fascia board. The board has been decorated with the same fabric as that of the curtains, and extends down behind the ruffle but in front of the track.*

pole, the further it can go without a central support, but even a full-sized pole may need one if it is required to carry heavy curtains.

Fixing track

The height at which track is fixed depends on the look you want and whether there is to be a pelmet. It can be attached either to the wall or to the ceiling.

Track is attached to the wall by brackets which can be either of fixed size or extendable to the required length. Supplied with track kits or bought separately, extendable brackets are useful if you want the curtain to stand clear of a blind or net curtain that will hang behind it. They can be screwed directly to the wall or to a wooden batten fixed to the wall, which will spread the load. Special brackets also allow more than one track for a layered effect.

Track should be fitted at least 5cm (2in) above the window and 15–40cm (6–16in) beyond either side of the window. To fix it, first screw the brackets to the wall, making sure they are level and spaced at regular intervals. Use a hacksaw to cut either plastic or metal track to the exact measurement you require. Clip the track to the brackets and then secure it to the wall according to the manufacturer's instructions.

Fixing poles and tracks

1 Poles are held by matching brackets, screwed onto the wall. Use wall plugs if fixing onto a masonry wall.

2 To fix track, draw a horizontal line with a spirit level to show the drilling position for the supporting brackets.

3 Pelmet boards are supported by right-angled brackets screwed to the underside, behind the curtain track.

4 To conceal the curtain track, make a small fascia board and cover it with the same fabric as the curtain.

When the window has a pelmet or a similar covering, the track can be attached either to the wall or to the base of the pelmet board. Its position should be far enough back from the front edge to allow room for bunching of the curtains when they are drawn open, but not so far back that the track is visible when looking up at the pelmet. The exact position depends on the bulkiness of the curtains. For unlined cotton curtains the track can be only 5cm (2in) from the front; heavy, interlined curtains will need to be hung further back.

Track can also be hidden when the curtains are drawn open by use of a fascia board attached to the front of a pelmet board. This is a narrow piece of wood or buckram, faced with the curtain material and attached with Velcro, tacks or glue around the edge of a pelmet board or to the front of the track. The track is fixed behind it to the pelmet board or wall; the curtain hooks loop into the runners, and the gathered frill of the curtains stands up in front of the fascia board to cover it when the curtains are closed.

Returns

To exclude light and draughts properly, curtains on track may need a return. This is a permanently fixed section of the curtain that blocks out the gap between the end of the track and the wall. If the track is attached to the wall by short brackets, very little light and few draughts will get through, and so a return may not be necessary. If the brackets are longer, make a fixing for the end of the curtain with an eyelet screw. If there is no pelmet board, either fix a block of wood to the wall for this purpose or use a special track return kit. This includes an arm which goes at a right angle to the end of the track and into which the curtain is hooked. Alternatively, plastic track with a metal core can be bent back to create a return.

Directory of fabrics

There is a vast range of fabrics suitable for curtains and blinds. Before choosing one, it is a good idea to spend some time in a well-stocked fabric shop or department, during daylight hours. Take any fabrics you particularly like the look of to the window to see their colour and finish in natural light; artificial lighting alters colours considerably. The shop will give you a tiny piece to take away. You can order a larger sample of anything you really like, but you will probably have to pay a deposit for this.

When you are ready to buy your fabric, take your measurements and calculations with you in case you need to consult an assistant about quantities. Be sure to buy enough fabric in one go, rather than having to go back later for more, as colour quality may not be identical between batches.

The following descriptions will help you decide which fabric is right for the curtain effect you want.

1

2

Sheer fabrics

Sheer and flimsy fabrics are suitable for curtains intended to diffuse and filter light as well as create privacy during daylight hours. They are too delicate to form blinds, but you can hang a plain, ungathered panel at the window. They can be combined with a heavier curtain in front, a blind behind or a frame formed by a lambrequin.

Pretty and elegant, voile is a very fine, sheer fabric printed or woven with a pattern or pictures. Ordinary nylon net comes with a ready-made hem down one side and a channel for inserting wire down the other and is sold in different widths. Lace makes a charming window covering, especially if you can find a picture panel or antique piece that fits your window. Embroidered cotton is a charming patterned alternative to lace or voile. Muslin, a loosely woven fine cotton, is less see-through than other sheers. It drapes well but crushes easily. 1

Plain fabrics

Unpatterned twill is usually a pure cotton fabric with subtly interesting textured weaves; the most attractive of which are, arguably, the herringbone and waffle patterns. Slubby fabric is often hand-woven and therefore has irregular threads which give it an attractive roughness.

Calico, available in various widths including some wide enough to curtain most windows without joins, is an inexpensive plain cotton fabric suitable for customizing, but wash it first to shrink it and remove the dressing before applying any paint.

Pure linen, and linen-and-cotton mixes known as linen union, are strong, long-lasting and hard-wearing fabrics which take dye superbly and hang well. Available in various weights, they look marvellous made up into curtains and blinds. 4

Checks and stripes

Of all patterns, checks and stripes are the most cheerful and unfussy. There is a huge variety of designs and colours available, and they generally mix well together in a room, especially alongside a traditional print such as floral linen or *toile de Jouy* (see opposite).

4

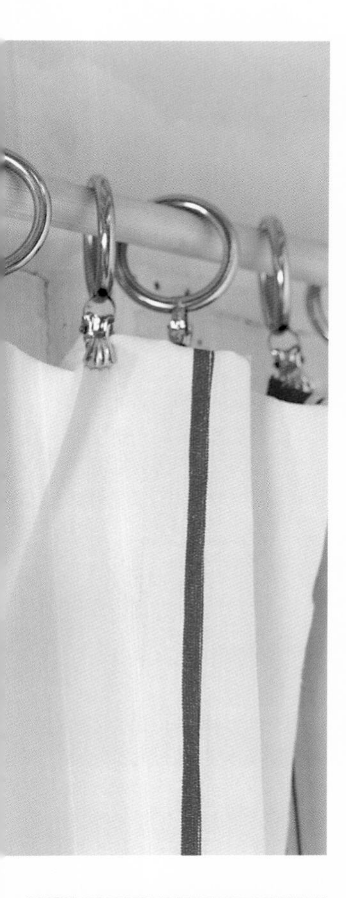

5

3

Geometric patterns always look good made into blinds, although they must be printed straight and cut square for a successful result.

Gingham is a jolly check formed from coloured stripes woven on a white background. Available in a dazzling range of alternatives, checks can be anything from quiet, woven in two subtle shades, to loud and boisterous, combining several bright colours. Madras cotton is a brightly patterned cotton check originally from India.

Wide stripes can look stunning and create a strong graphic image when formed into a blind, draped over a pole across the top of the window or made into floor-length curtains. 2

Narrow stripes are more restrained and will contribute a quiet elegance to an interior. They mix well with floral prints and checks in the same colour range. Horizontal stripes are less common than vertical ones, but they do have many of the same qualities, although they will not help a dull, low window look any taller.

Originally designed to keep feathers inside mattresses, ticking has a distinctive stripe. It is available in variously coloured stripes on white or cream, and has become popular as an inexpensive and hard-wearing soft-furnishing fabric.

Traditional patterned fabrics

Due to their long history and historical associations, traditional fabrics add a certain grace and gravitas to a room. They also remain among the most beautiful patterned fabrics available.

Floral prints are quintessentially English. Among the most charming are those that have a faded look, as if they have been around for generations. Florals mix well with other patterns, such as stripes, which can freshen them up and prevent them looking fusty. Chintz, a glazed cotton printed with flowers such as roses and peonies, is the epitome of English style. 3

Toile de Jouy is a distinctive picture fabric, generally showing pastoral scenes, printed in a single colour on white or cream.

Provençal prints, based originally on imported seventeenth-century Indian-printed fabrics, are decorated with flowers and abstract motifs printed in black and distinctive rich colours like egg yolk and bottle green. They make a strong impact, combining a rustic farmhouse feel with the exoticism of Provençal heat, harsh sunlight and scented air.

Jacquard has a pattern woven into it, often of flowers and leaves, and a slightly silky finish.

Paisley, a popular fabric design that originated in Scotland, has a swirling pattern of rounded shapes that curve into a point; it generally comes in rich and strong colours. 5

1

2

Tartan, the Scottish hallmark beloved of Queen Victoria, who decorated whole rooms with it, has a sober, masculine feel. The colours are mostly rich and resonant, though some are rather drab and disappointing.

Graphic print fabrics

Sometimes sharply defined, sometimes loose and painterly, but generally fresh and uncluttered, images such as stars, heraldic motifs, circles, triangles and letters of the alphabet are favoured motifs for this sort of fabric. Colours vary from pale and subtle to knock-out brilliant. Many are manufactured in several colourways, with curtains in one colour, say, to be combined with a pelmet in another – the pattern being the unifying force.

Picture-print fabrics

These have picture images scattered across them and the best are wonderfully fresh and attractive. Because of their content, such as circus performers, boats, animals, cups and saucers, fruit and vegetables, classical motifs or playing cards, some are better used in one type of room than another. Some designed for children's rooms are particularly delightful. 2

Ethnic fabrics

These can add variety and interest to almost any style of interior, not only those with an ethnic feel. Indian crewelwork, woollen chain stitch worked on a creamy cotton background, usually depicts birds and leaves in light shades of blues, greens and pinks. Kilim print is strongly coloured printed cotton with bold and distinctive geometric patterns drawn from kilims, woven cotton and wool rugs made in central Asia. Hand-blocked Indian cotton can be fragile, so it needs to be handled with care.

Rich fabrics

These gorgeous fabrics are useful for creating a grand or sumptuous interior and an aura of luxury. Pure silk is the most lustrous of fabrics but varies greatly in type, quality and price. It is available in a dazzling choice of colours, some shot through with another colour, some overprinted with

4

3

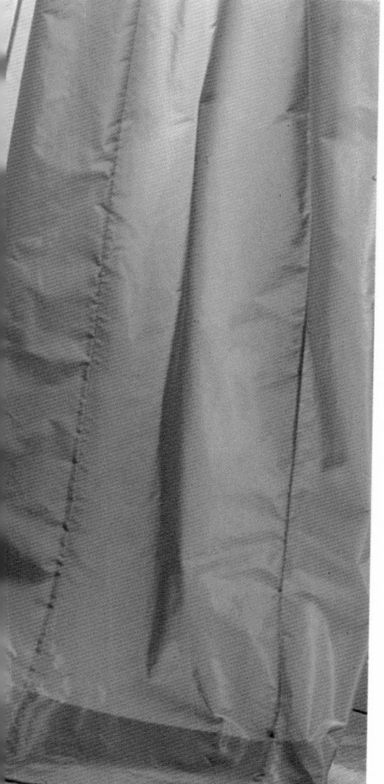

a pattern, some woven into checks or other patterns. Although it is not hardy enough for blind making and it rots in sunlight, it should not necessarily be excluded from curtain-making, but it must be used with care and forethought.

Damask can be made from silk, cotton or man-made fibres. It has a woven, two-tone pattern, usually of intertwined leaves and/or flowers. Really grand damask comes with appliqué and/or embroidery added to the surface. Like damask, brocade has a woven pattern but in more than the one colour.

Velvet, the most luxurious of fabrics, has a pile which must always lie in the same direction, otherwise the colour will look different. Available in a whole range of colours and patterns, it is incomparably sumptuous and invaluable for creating an atmosphere of comfort and elegance. The thickness of its pile makes it unsuitable for making into blinds. Plush has a pile like velvet, but it is longer and less closely woven. It was particularly popular in the nineteenth century for tablecloths and as curtains in a multi-layered window treatment.

Lining fabrics

Coloured linings are available in a range of colours to match or contrast with almost every fabric. Although some are certified fade-proof, the safest choice is always cream or white. There is also a choice of qualities, the best having a certain amount of body that will survive cleaning.

Blackout, a special fabric for excluding light, is available in various weights, the heaviest of which can be difficult to work with. Thermal lining, known as milium, is coated on one side with aluminium and gives excellent thermal protection without adding bulk to curtains in the way that interlinings do.

Interlinings

For luxuriously thick curtains that will drape well and provide good draught protection, use interlining. Bump, the heaviest, bulkiest type, makes curtains look luxurious. It gives excellent protection against cold and, indeed, heat, when sewn into curtains. Lighter domette can be used with lighter fabrics and gives body to Roman blinds and pelmets. Synthetic, the lightest of all, can be slightly see-through. Its main virtue is its cheapness, but its other good points are that it should not shrink when cleaned, and it will not cover you with fluff during sewing.

Trimmings

Interesting trimmings can transform a handsome curtain into something really special. A ribbon, 1.5cm (⅝in) or more wide, adds interest and definition if you choose a contrasting colour and set it back from the edges of a curtain or blind. Braid is a looped and woven trimming available in a multitude of colours and designs, some of which are wonders of textile engineering and fiercely expensive. A braid with pompoms, sewn along the leading edges of a pair of simple muslin or sheer curtains, will completely transform them. Fringing, too, comes in endless variations of colour and design. One of its best uses is at the bottom of an Austrian blind or pull-up curtain (see pages 74–75). When the blind is pulled up, the fringe looks pretty against the light; when let down, it gives weight and definition to the bottom edge. A pelmet or blind with a shaped bottom edge can be made to look positively exotic if tassels are attached to hang off each downward point. Some ready-made edgings incorporate beading. Alternatively, you can sew or string individual beads along the edge of a sheer curtain for added weight, detail and a delicate touch of colour. 3

First steps to making curtains

Measuring up and estimating quantities

Measuring up a window and estimating how much fabric is required for the curtains need to be done accurately. To work out how much fabric you need, the formula is to multiply the number of fabric widths required by the working length of the curtains, plus any allowance for a pattern repeat. For how to determine these lengths, see below.

Having established the style of your curtains, it is easiest to take the measurements for your fabric once you have installed the pole and rings or track and runners (see pages 42–43) from which they will hang. Tracks and poles must be fixed with enough room either side of the window to accommodate the curtains when pulled back (heavy fabrics will need more than light fabrics), and should be fixed at least 5cm (2in) above the window.

If you want to purchase your fixings and fabric at the same time, you must estimate the positioning of your track or pole and the depth of any rings as accurately as you can.

Since you will not know the width of your fabric, or the size of any pattern repeat, until you have chosen it, you will have to do most of your calculations in the shop. Take your measurements and a calculator.

▲ *A wall of light-flooded windows is curtained with a sheer lightweight fabric edged with bands of colour in a slightly heavier fabric. Joining widths to make wide curtains is much easier if the fabric has no pattern, but the seams must be neat on both sides if the fabric is see-through.*

Measuring for fabric widths

To calculate the number of widths of fabric you need, first measure the length of the pole or track (A) (not the window). For a track with an overlap in the middle, add on the amount of the overlap. Add as much as necessary to cover any returns at the sides (from the track back to the wall).

Multiply this curtain-width measurement (A) by the multiple required for your chosen curtain heading (see pages 52–53). Add 7.5cm (3in) per curtain (i.e. 15cm/6in for a pair) to allow for turnbacks, then divide this figure by the given width of your chosen fabric. The resulting figure is the number of widths of fabric you need. Round up to the nearest whole number of widths. (If your figure is only just over a whole number, you might consider rounding down rather than up because of the large amount of wastage involved, especially if your fabric is costly.)

Measuring for working length

The length of fabric depends on the chosen length of the curtains, plus any allowance for the hanging, depending on how much it will be covered by the top of the curtains.

For a pole and rings that will be totally in view, measure from the bottom of a curtain ring. If, however, you want a ruffle to cover part of the rings, start from where the top of the ruffle will be.

For a track, which should be hidden when the curtains are closed, measure from just above the top edge of the track. If the track is to be hidden by a pelmet, measure from the runners. If it is to have a fixed, non-drawing heading, measure from the top of the piece of wood across the top of the window to which the curtain will be attached. In all cases add 4cm (1½in) to allow for the turnover at the top of the curtains.

Measure down to the sill (B), below the sill (C) or to the floor (D). For curtains that

Measuring up for curtains

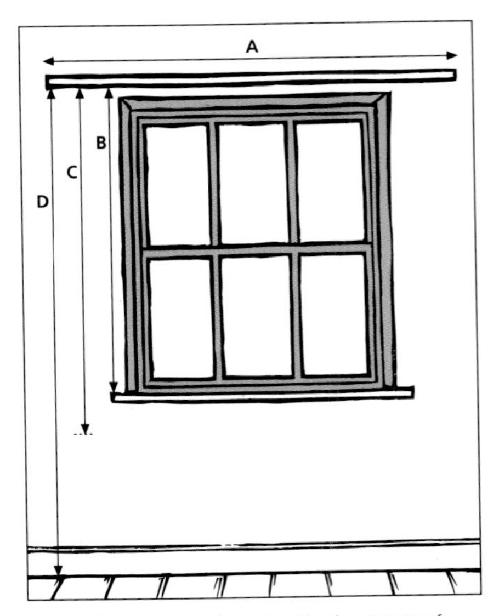

Curtain dimensions are determined by the amount of window clearance at either side and the length desired.

Tools and materials

For measuring up and fixing

- **Step ladder.**
- **Steel tape measure:** use a long metal tape rather than a fabric one which might have stretched with use, and measure in centimetres.
- **Notepad and pencil:** for recording the measurements.

All curtains

To make up curtains, plenty of space – ideally a large table – is essential. If the table is not large enough, lay a big board on it to provide a larger work area.

- **A sewing machine, and supply of needles:** any machine with a pedal action or electric pedal control will do so long as it does a straight running stitch.
- **Fabric, lining, interlining and trimming** (although all of the last three are optional).
- **Thread:** for tacking (in a dark colour if the fabric is light, light if it is dark); and also for sewing – plenty of it in a colour to match the front fabric. Always use thread of the same fibre and similar weight as the fabric itself.
- **Weights:** to help curtains hang well, weights can be inserted in the hem. Alternatively, a special weighted tape can be sewn on.
- **Sharp scissors:** in various sizes.
- **Dressmaker's pins:** these must be sharp and rust-free. Glass-headed ones are more easily noticeable and less likely to get lost in the curtain. Do not leave pins in fabric for long as they might leave holes.
- **Tailor's chalk:** for marking cutting lines.
- **Steam iron:** to press material flat before and after making up.

Keep your sewing equipment orderly, tidying up at the end of each day so that you can find things when you start again. A tray or box in which to keep all loose equipment is useful. Heavy weights for holding fabric in place, such as bricks wrapped in scrap interlining and sewn into scrap cotton, are a good idea. Sew a handle on the top of each for easy lifting and moving as you work.

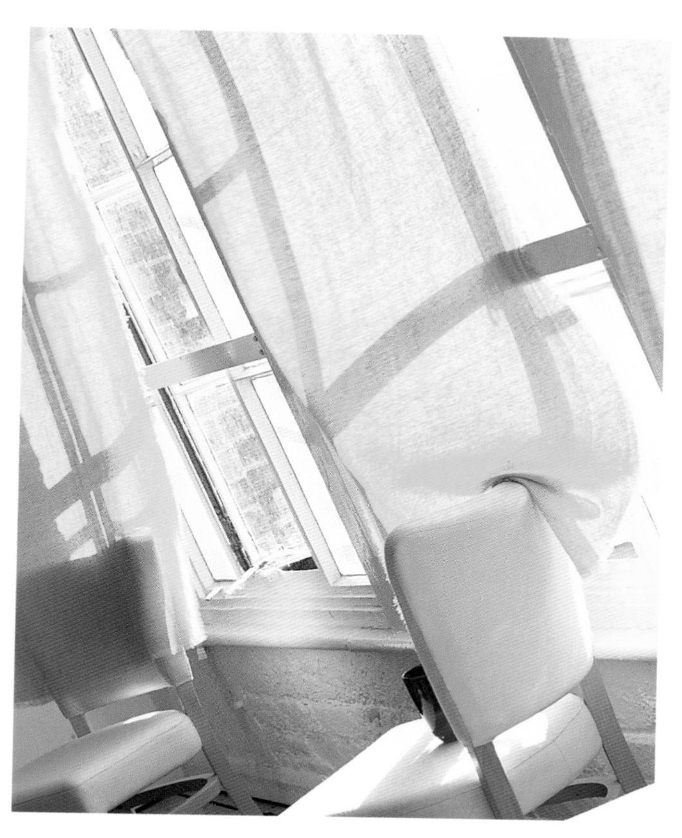

◀ *Where there is a large expanse of window, an economical and contemporary option is to have curtains which hang completely flat when closed. These can be made specially or ready-made textiles such as shawls, throws or tablecloths can be used for instant effect.*

will drape on the floor add 15–25cm (6–10in), depending on how much curtain you want on the floor; for ones that will just skim the floor deduct 6mm (¼in). Finally, add a hem allowance of 16cm (6½in) for lined curtains or 10cm (4in) for unlined.The total figure is the working length of the curtain.

Pattern repeats

Patterned fabrics have a 'repeat', the distance between the point where the pattern begins and the point where it ends before being repeated. When a fabric has a repeat, you will need to allow extra fabric in order to match the pattern across joined widths of a curtain and also across two curtains. To calculate the extra fabric needed, round up the working length of the curtain to the nearest whole multiple of the repeat measurement. For example, if the working length is 1.95m (76¾in) and the repeat is 20cm (8in), round the working length figure up to the next multiple of 20cm (8in), i.e. 2m (78¾in).

▲ *Another economical method of covering large windows is to hang curtains made from different fabrics whose colour and texture contrast interestingly, all finished to the same length. The fabrics might be inexpensive in themselves, like the blue cheesecloth here, or bought cheaply in sales or as remnants.*

Cutting, matching and joining fabric

▲ *A simple yellow-and-white striped cotton has been cleverly transformed by dividing the curtains into bands with the stripes going alternately down and across. The bands of fabric are separated by a narrow black stripe. For added visual interest, a checked Roman blind hangs behind each pair of curtains.*

Cutting fabric

Iron the fabric smooth to make it easier to measure. Cut this to the individual lengths you require, ensuring that both top and bottom raw edges are cut straight – at 90 degrees to the selvedges. With loosely woven fabric and linens, a weft (crossways) thread can be drawn out enabling you to cut along the line left by it in the fabric. For other fabrics you will need to use a set square.

Plain fabric

Measure out your lengths, marking each cutting line with pins at each side on the selvedge. If necessary, use a metre (yard) stick to align the two marks and, using tailor's chalk, draw a line to cut across the fabric. As you cut each length, mark the top of the fabric with a safety pin. Fold each length neatly or roll it onto a cardboard tube to prevent it getting creased or crumpled. If you are making two curtains, then you will need to divide the number of widths in half at this point (e.g. 4 widths = 2 curtains of 2 widths each; 3 widths = 2 curtains of 1½ widths each). The total width of fabric you need rarely coincides with an exact number of fabric widths. If the discrepancy is small, it may be preferable to absorb some extra width by taking it up in the curtain heading. Certainly for unlined, fine fabric, distributing excess fabric in the spacing of the folds as it hangs is less of a problem than for a heavy fabric with a box-pleated heading.

If you do need to remove excess fabric, trim a width at the outside or back edge of each curtain, never at the inside or leading edge. Similarly, if a width of fabric is being split into two to make up the required total width, add the part width to the outside or back edge in the same way.

Patterned fabric

Before you start work, check for faults and misprinting. The fabric should be cut following the grain. If the pattern is not square to the selvedge or is printed off the grain, consider returning it to the shop or adjust your cutting to follow the pattern.

Try to arrange a patterned fabric so that the bottom of the curtain falls at the end of a repeat. Mark a line across the fabric along the base of the first pattern repeat, then mark a second line for the hem allowance – 16cm (6½in) below for lined curtains, 10cm (4in) for unlined. Cut on this second line. For full-length curtains that are to hang from a pole, where the pattern will be less gathered up than when using heading tape, you might prefer to have the complete repeat at the top. In this case, you will need to measure your lengths from the top of the fabric downwards. Draw your first line across the fabric at the top of the first pattern repeat, then a second line 4cm (1½in) above that for the heading allowance. Cut on the second line.

It is important that the pattern matches across the widths and across both curtains if there are two. Line up the first cut length against the uncut fabric, matching the pattern exactly before cutting a second length.

Joining widths

Plain fabric

To join the drops, pin right sides together along the edge. Tack along each seam then sew, 1.5cm (⅝in) in from the edge, from the bottom. Press flat. For unlined curtains, you can make a flat fell seam. Having pressed the seam flat, trim back one seam allowance to half its original width. Fold the other one over to cover it, then fold under this edge of the seam allowance to enclose the raw edges. Top stitch through all the layers. This will show on the front of the curtain.

Patterned fabric

To join patterned fabric, fold under and press a 1.5cm (⅝in) seam allowance down the side that is to be joined of one length of fabric. With right sides facing upwards, place this over the unfolded seam allowance of the second piece, matching the pattern horizontally and pinning it in place. This should be tacked using ladder stitch. With a knotted thread starting under the fold, stitch up through the fabric and across the join and down through the bottom piece and back up through the fold. Repeat to form horizontal 'ladder' stitches across the join. To machine stitch the seam, place the right sides of the fabric together and stitch in the usual way.

Cutting, matching and joining fabric

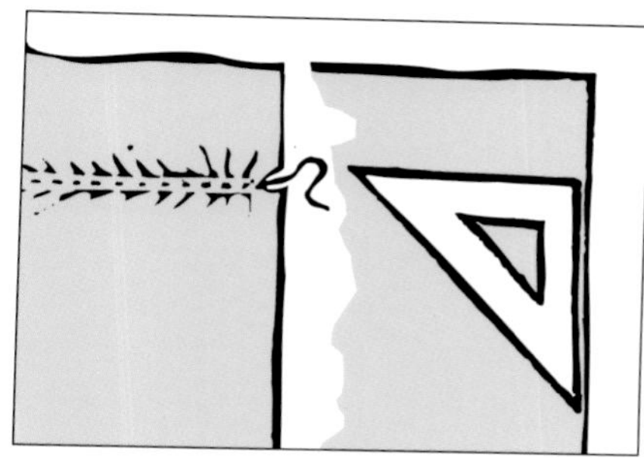

1 *To get a straight, right-angled raw edge, pull out a weft thread, if possible, or place a set square on the selvedge.*

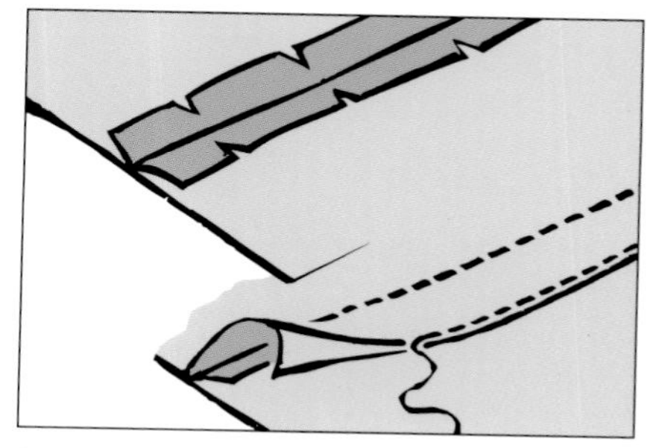

2 *Either press seams open, or trim back one side, fold over the other to enclose the raw edges and top stitch.*

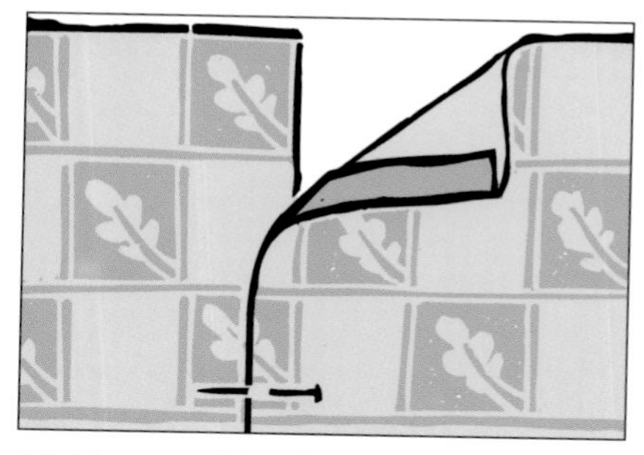

3 *To join patterned fabric, fold under one seam allowance, place it over the other, matching the pattern, and pin.*

4 *Hand sew in place with a ladder stitch, then turn the top piece back and machine stitch along the seam line.*

▲ *In this grand window treatment, fixed linen curtains have a cased heading made from the same bold stripe as the blind behind, and the linen has been carefully matched to ensure the pattern works perfectly across the seams. The static heading allows the curtains to drape beautifully, and the decorative pole and finials complete the effect.*

Gathered headings

The way that the top of the curtain is gathered or folded into a pattern of pleats is referred to as the 'curtain heading'. The type of heading affects how the fabric falls when the curtains are closed as well as the amount of fabric required to make the curtains.

For substantially interlined, heavyweight curtains, the heading is best made by hand, with the pleats and hooks sewn in individually. This is a job for a professional or someone with experience of making curtains. The usual way for amateurs and beginners to arrange the top of curtains is to use ready-made, woven heading tape.

Heading tapes vary in depth and stiffness, according to the type of gather. They have strings threaded through them for gathering up the curtain, and pockets into which the hooks - by which the curtains are suspended from the pole or track - are inserted. An alternative to pull-cord tapes are those tapes with which you use prongs to form the gathering. These are easily removed for cleaning.

Heading tape is sold by the metre (yard). The length required is a little more than the total fabric width required for each curtain.

Types of heading tape

Different multiples of fabric are suggested for the tapes listed below. The range of multiples for some tapes allows a choice between the minimum amount of fabric required to make the heading look respectable and the maximum amount for a generous look.

Standard: This tape gives a shallow, gently gathered heading suitable for lightweight, unlined curtains. Depending on how full the curtains are to be, the fabric width required is 1½ to 2 times the length of the pole or track. The tape should be sewn 2.5cm (1in) from the top of the curtain – so that the curtain will cover any tracking or partly cover the rings of a pole – or it can be sewn closer to the top to allow it to hang below the rings on a pole.

Pencil pleat: Wider and more robust than standard heading tape, this gives a much deeper, smarter, more regimented gather, pulling the fabric into regular, rounded pencil-shaped pleats. Suitable for most types of curtain, it is available in several widths and requires a fabric width of 2¼ to 2½ times the length of the track or pole. There are three

▶ *The triple-pleat heading, also known as a French or pinch pleat, is fixed in place on this small window, giving the curtains a handsome finish. Having fixed curtains is a practical choice in this situation, as there is no space on the right into which the curtain could be drawn back.*

Gathered headings

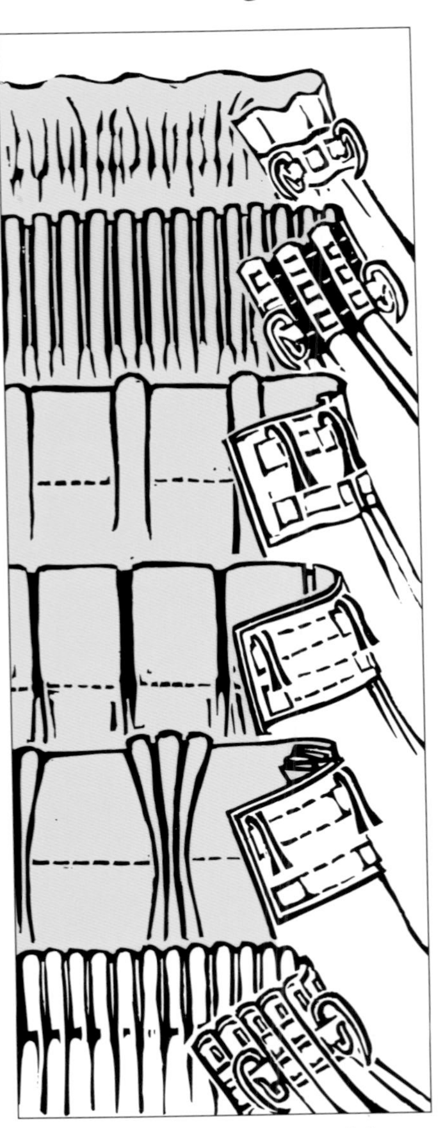

Headings with tape (from top): standard, pencil pleat, cartridge pleat, box pleat, triple/pinch pleat and net pleat.

Heading tape

1 Turn under the heading allowance, place the tape in position and knot the strings under the cord.

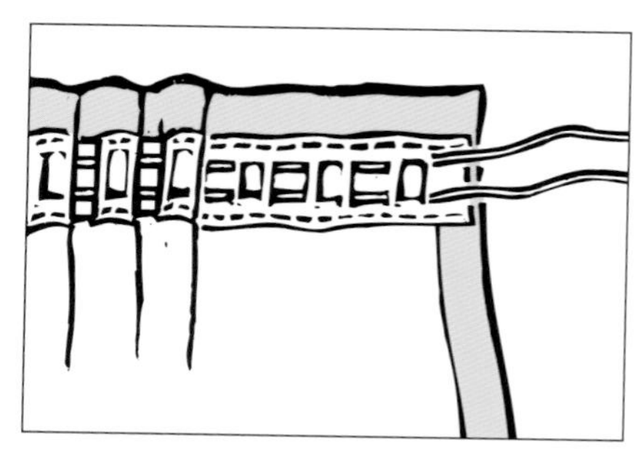

2 Hold the free cords in one hand and push the heading along until it is pleated to the required amount.

3 Insert hooks at each end and space the rest evenly along the curtain; tie the strings around a cord tidy.

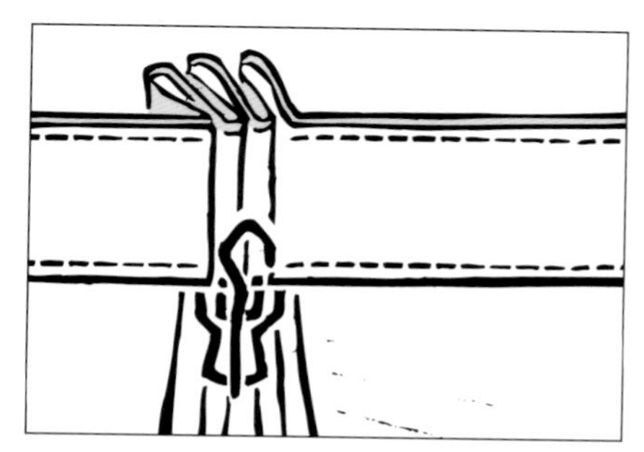

4 For triple pleats, insert one prong of a pleater hook in each of the four pockets. Skip one pocket, then repeat.

rows of pockets, to offer a choice of hanging heights. The tape should be sewn 3mm (⅛in) from the top of the curtain.

Cartridge pleat: Cartridge pleats are single, large, regular, rounded pleats spaced between flat stretches of fabric. They give curtains sophistication, especially heavy floor-length ones. When pulling up the tape, match the pleats evenly across both curtains if there is a pair. Avoid having a pleat at either leading or back edge; these should hang flat. Cartridge pleats require a fabric width of 2½ times the length of the track or pole. The tape should be sewn 3mm (⅛in) from the top of the curtain.

Box pleat: Like cartridge-pleat tape, this tape gives regular, tailored pleats, but these are flat and tucked behind the flat fabric rather than in front of it. Box pleats are suitable for all types of curtain, especially heavy, lined ones. When pulling up the tape, match the pleats evenly across both curtains if there is a pair. Box pleats require 3 times the length of track or pole, and the tape should be sewn 3mm (⅛in) from the top of the curtain.

Triple or pinch pleat: This tape gives regular, fanned, triple pleats at intervals across the curtain. Known as French pleats, these produce a handsome, tailored look for formal lined curtains and are available in several depths. When pulling up the tape, match the pleats evenly across both curtains if there is a pair. This tape requires fabric twice the length of the track or pole and should be sewn 3mm (⅛in) from the top of the curtain.

Net: This is a discreet, lightweight tape for net or sheer fabrics, combining pockets for hooks and loops for wire. It can be sewn to the top of the curtain either way up, depending on how much of the curtain you want to stand up above the hooks. Alternatively, wire or a rod can be threaded through the loops. Net tape can take a fabric width 2 to 3 three times the length of the wire, pole or track.

Attaching heading tape

Heading tape is sewn onto the top of the curtain back, once the curtain has been made. Lay the tape over the raw edge of the turnback (see left for position) and pin and tack in place. At the inside edge of the curtain, unthread the strings for about 2.5cm (1in), then knot them underneath. Fold the tape end under to cover the knots; tack in place. Repeat on the outside edge of the curtain, but leave the cords free and on top of the tape. Machine stitch the tape in the same direction along both edges to avoid puckering. Machine stitch over both the tape ends, making sure the needle doesn't pass through the strings at the outside edge.

▲ An otherwise plain triple-pleat curtain heading has been given the added decorative detail of a self-covered button on each of the pleats. This accentuates the pleats, but in a restrained way. The narrow curtain rod is carefully placed above the window to ensure it does not mask the charming plaster roses on the cornice.

Gathering

Gather the curtain by holding the loose strings and pushing the tape along until it is sufficiently pleated to measure the length of the pole (for a single curtain) or half the length (for a pair). If you are using track with an overlap, allow for this. Coil then knot the loose strings or wrap them around a cord tidy (see page 41). You can then insert the hooks, one at each end of the curtain with others spaced evenly between them.

Handmade headings

Headings can be created for hanging curtains from poles without using a heading tape. They include pierced headings, looped, tie-on and cased headings. Except for cased headings, each of the headings described below needs to have a loop, eyelet or tie at or very near each top corner to prevent the ends from drooping. When buying fabric for a curtain with looped headings you will need the same width of fabric as the length of the pole, and for pierced and tied headings, approximately twice the length of the pole, depending on the fabric and the way you wish the folds to hang. If in doubt, ask for advice at the point of purchase.

▲ *Cheerful, cottagey sunshine-yellow gingham curtains, unlined to let in the light, have been teamed with an interesting heading. An integral valance adds weight to the heading, while extra-long fabric ties are both functional – attaching the curtain to the pole – and decorative, hanging down rather like ribbons.*

Pierced heading

Pierced curtains have metal-rimmed eyelets inserted along the top of the curtain through which a thin pole is threaded. Use an inexpensive eyelet kit bought from a DIY or hardware store. The eyelets should be positioned on the wrong side of the hem, approximately 10cm (4in) apart.

If you are using an eyelet kit, practise on a spare piece of fabric before making the holes in the curtains. Place the fabric over the die provided with the kit and, using the narrow end of the tool and a hammer, punch a small hole in it. Assemble both parts of the eyelet around the hole. The washer part should be uppermost, on the wrong side of the material, with its closed side upwards. Using the wide end of the tool, hit the washer sharply with a hammer. When you feel confident enough to make the eyelets in the curtain, use the position marks you have made on the curtain to line up the eyelet tool. To avoid later ripping of the fabric, the top of the curtain can be reinforced first with binding, cotton webbing or ribbon.

Looped heading

A looped heading has lined fabric tabs sewn into the top of the curtain through which the pole is slotted. Bearing in mind the total width of the curtain, determine how many tabs you want and their width. The finished width of each should be approximately 5cm (2in), so to make them, double the width and add 3cm (1¼in) for a seam. To establish how long the tabs need to be, measure the circumference of the rod or pole and then add 5cm (2in) for ease, plus 3cm (1¼in) for seams.

Cut out the strips of fabric and fold them in half lengthways, right sides together, and sew 1.5cm (⅝in) seams. Turn the tubes right side out and press them flat with the seam in the middle of one side. Loop the tabs and sew them together with a 1.5cm (⅝in) seam. Sew them to the right side of the fabric, 1.5cm (⅝in) from the top and with the loops hanging down.

Cut a strip of fabric for the facing 7.5cm (3in) deep and the same width as the curtain, plus 3cm (1¼in). Sew a small hem along one long edge of this. With right sides facing, pin the other, unhemmed edge to the curtain, along the attachment line of the loops, 1.5cm (⅝in) from the top edge. Tack and then stitch this strip in place along the top edge, catching in the loop bases as you go. Sew small hems at each end of the strip so that the strip aligns perfectly with the curtain.

Fold the facing strip over to the back of the curtain, with the wrong sides

Headings without tapes

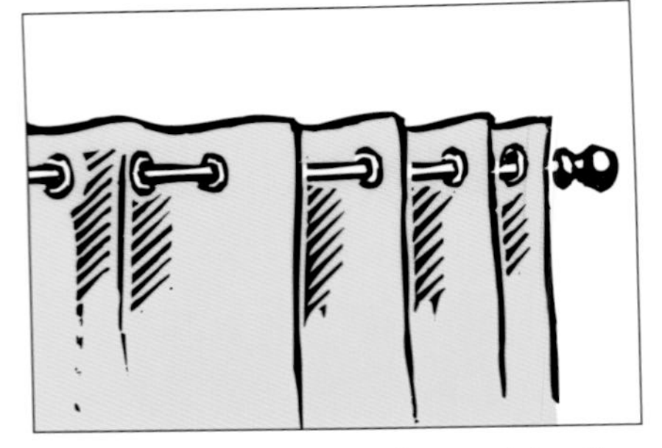

A1 *A pierced curtain has metal eyelets spaced along the top, and the curtain is threaded onto a narrow pole.*

B1 *Tabs of fabric are looped over and sewn onto the top of the curtain. A facing strip covers the seam line.*

C1 *A variation on the looped heading is the tied-on curtain, where fabric strips are tied into bows.*

D1 *A cased or slotted heading can be sited at the top of the curtain or set down to form a ruffle.*

Making the headings

A2 *Using an eyelet kit, place the fabric over the die, and hit the narrow end of the tool with a hammer.*

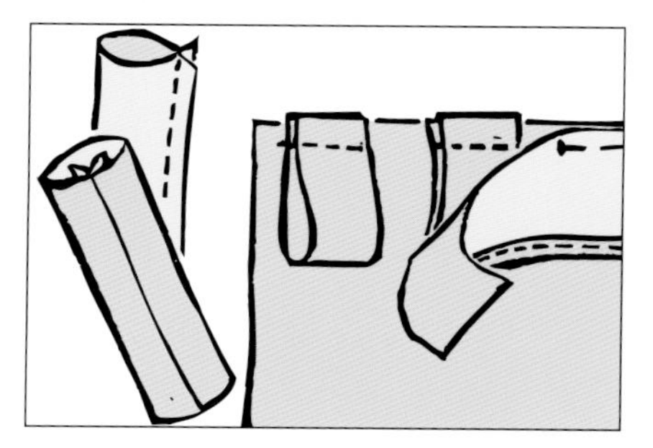

B2 *Fold strips of fabric in half and seam. Place along top of curtain, stitch in place, then cover with facing strip.*

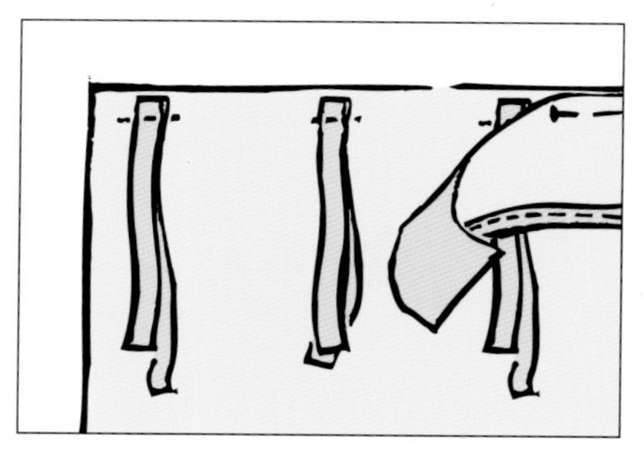

C2 *Stitch pairs of ties evenly across the curtain top, then cover with a facing strip as for the looped heading.*

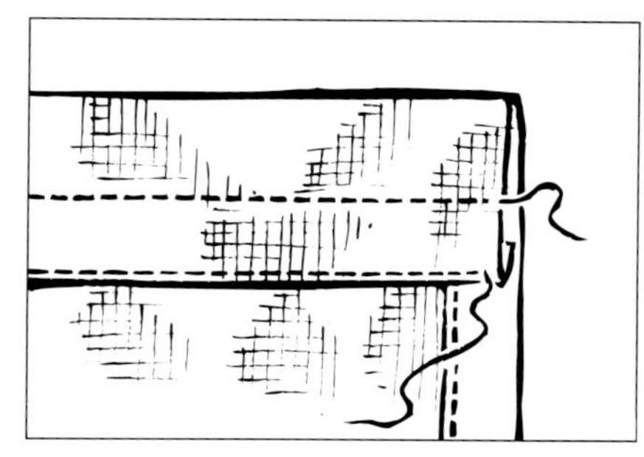

D2 *Fold a double hem deep enough for the slot and frill (if wanted) and stitch on either side of the slot.*

together. Press so that the loops stand up at the top of the curtain. Slip stitch along the bottom edge and sides of the facing.

Tie-on curtains

Ties can be sewn into the top of the curtain in the same manner as the tabs of a looped heading and tied around a pole. Loose ties – made of ribbon, raffia, string, or 'invisible' fishing line – could be inserted through the eyelets of a pierced curtain instead of a pole.

Cased heading

A cased heading (also known as a slotted heading) is made by forming a channel or slot to take the curtain pole. At its simplest this can be made at the very top of the curtain heading, or it can be placed just down from the top of the curtain so that a ruffle stands up above it. For this, fold a double hem deep enough for the slot and any frill, and first tack and then machine stitch along either side of the slot, in the same direction. The size of the slot is dictated by the diameter of the pole, which should fit easily, without the fabric being too tight or slack. You need a total fabric width of up to 2½ times the length of the pole, plus turnbacks. Curtains with cased headings cannot be drawn back easily, so they are well suited to sheers or nets which are intended to hang down permanently or be draped to one side.

▲ *These stunning gauzy linen curtains have been given texture and interest by making horizontal pleats throughout their length. The pleats, which hang loose, are quite narrow at the top and increasingly wide as they approach the bottom. The curtains have cased headings at the top and drape on the floor.*

Other headings

For lightweight curtains, make a double hem at the top edge and simply sew small brass rings at intervals along it for threading onto a pole. Alternatively, you can buy special curtain clips – essentially rings with decorative clips at the bottom – which clip onto the top of the curtain (see page 41).

No-sew curtains

It is possible to make curtains without sewing a single stitch. All you need are tools and materials such as fabric glue, pinking shears, hammer and nails or a staple gun and staples, an eyelet tool or curtain clips. For curtains that make use of either of the latter two items, fold and glue a wide ribbon or tape over the raw edge at the top of the fabric to finish and reinforce it.

For all these curtains, use a fabric that is wide enough to cover the window without needing joins and, if possible, one that has a self-coloured selvedge. You can leave the edges plain or you can cut, turn back and glue decorative borders such as zigzag, scallop or castellated patterns.

Draped fabric

A very simple curtain style consists of a length of fabric, twice the height of the window, just thrown over a pole, with one or both layers draped to one side. To prevent the curtain sliding along the pole, reinforce and nail or staple the fabric at intervals to it.

Unlined curtains and sheers

Although they are often considered the poor relations of the curtain world, unlined curtains are among the most versatile, and in the right situation they can be beautiful. A single thickness of lightweight fabric will not excel at excluding light or draughts, but it has its own positive qualities. It will drape easily over a hold-back or on the floor. It can diffuse sunshine, creating privacy without blocking the light, and it can make an important contribution to a layered window treatment.

Natural fabrics

Linen, cotton twill, slub cotton and calico all work well when made into unlined curtains, as do lightweight, purpose-made textiles such as striped cotton sheets, Indian hand-printed cotton bedspreads and saris with glittering woven borders (but remember that pure silk fades and even rots in sunlight). You can create your own decoration on an unlined cotton curtain by painting or drawing on it with special fabric paints or pens.

Sheers

Net, voile, lace and muslin are not intended to be lined, so they can be used to veil a window rather than to cover it up. They can be difficult to handle, especially if they are made from certain man-made fibres. If you find that they are slippery, try placing strips of tissue paper between the two layers you are sewing together and under the sewing machine foot; you simply tear the paper away afterwards. Use lightweight thread with sheers. Some of these fabrics have a top and bottom hem already sewn into them and are sold off rolls in different lengths to suit the heights of standard window sizes. Just buy the amount you need for the width of your window.

▶▶ Two layers of muslin, each a different brilliant colour, are sewn together across the top to create a magical curtain which drapes and billows beautifully. Natural fibres such as cotton can be dyed colourfast at home in a washing machine with household dyes.

▶ The single, flat, white unlined curtain that masks this window can be draped back to either side during the day. Braid strung with ornaments, laid flat across the top, adds visual interest and reduces the curtain's starkness and severity.

Washing unlined curtains

Unlined curtains can be washed, a process not advised for lined curtains because the different fabrics shrink at different rates. A sensible idea is to pre-wash the fabric so that

any shrinkage happens before you make the curtains. The disadvantage of this, however, is that you remove the finish or dressing that helps protect it from gathering dust.

An alternative to pre-washing is to cut the curtain extra wide and long, so that it drapes on the floor, gather it tightly at the top when first hung, and wash it only when absolutely necessary. When you rehang it, any shrinkage in the length will be absorbed by the billowing bottom, and you can gather the width less tightly across the top.

Making the curtains

Unlined curtains are the easiest curtains of all to make yourself, especially if you have chosen a fabric that is easy to handle. With sufficiently wide fabric you may not even have to join drops, just hem around the edges and sew on heading tape or rings. If you do have to join drops, remember that the seams will be seen on the back of the curtain. You can use an open flat seam, but a French or flat fell seam that turns the raw edge in will give a much neater finish.

Once the widths are joined and any excess at the sides trimmed, turn in and press a double 2cm (¾in) hem on each side of the curtain and a double 5cm (2in) hem along the bottom, inserting leadweight tape (special weighted tape) if you want to give the fabric a bit of added weight.

To mitre the corners (which gives a neat, short diagonal seam where the side and bottom hems meet), unfold one turn of both the bottom and side hems but mark the limit of the double turns with pins on the edge. Fold the corner up diagonally, through the corner point of the curtain and the points marked with a pin. Refold the bottom and side hems to form a neat mitre. Finish these hems and the diagonal join with slip stitch. Do not cut the fabric across the corner, because it's possible that you will want to alter the curtains in the future.

Measure the finished curtain length up from the hem and mark the line with pins. Turn over the excess at the top, folding in the sides at a slight angle as you do so to form a neat edge. Press it and then trim back the fabric if necessary so that the heading tape will cover the raw edge. Snip the hems at each side on the fold line to ease the material. Attach the heading tape and gather up the curtains (see pages 52–53).

You are now ready to hang the curtain on its track or pole. The outermost hook on each curtain goes into a fixed hole to anchor it in place. This is either an eyelet screwed into the pelmet board or into a wall-mounted wooden block, or the end hole in a track; alternatively, on a curtain pole, it is the ring on the pole between the end bracket and the finial.

Making unlined curtains

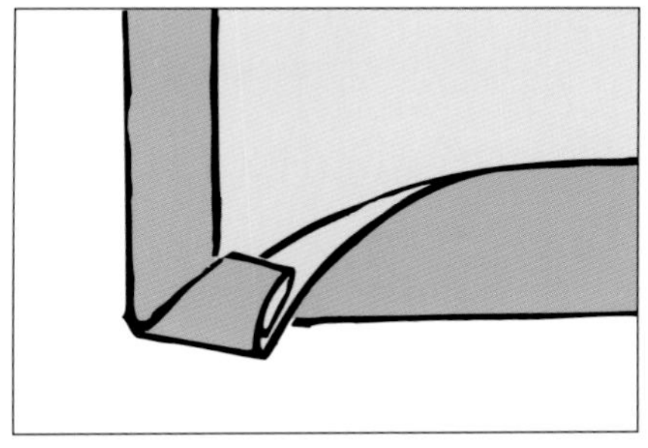

1 *Turn a double 2cm (¾in) hem at each side and a double 5cm (2in) hem along the bottom. Press.*

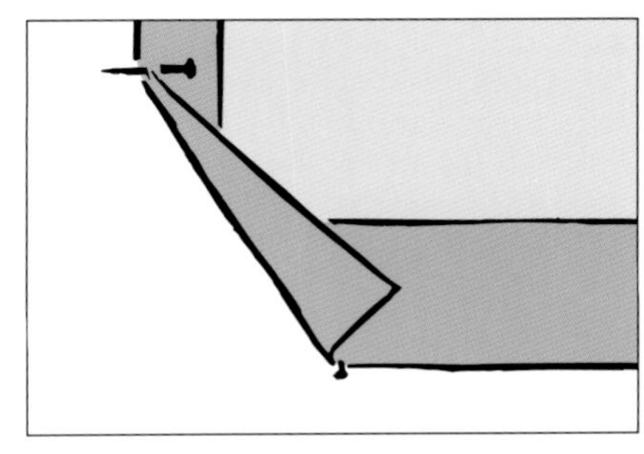

2 *Open out one fold and mark the limit of the double hems with pins. Fold diagonally through both pins.*

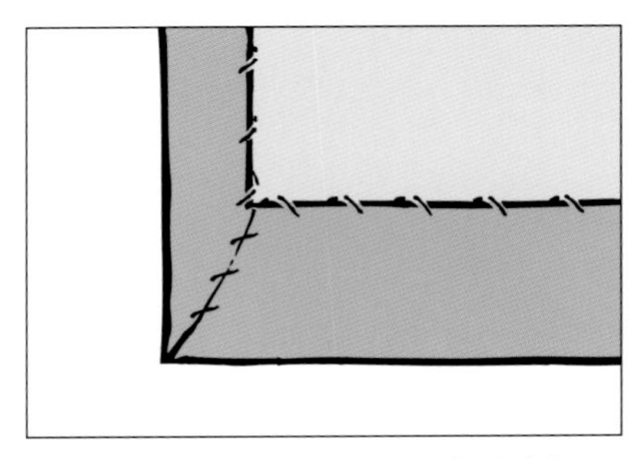

3 *Refold the edges to form a mitre, and slip stitch the diagonal join and both hems.*

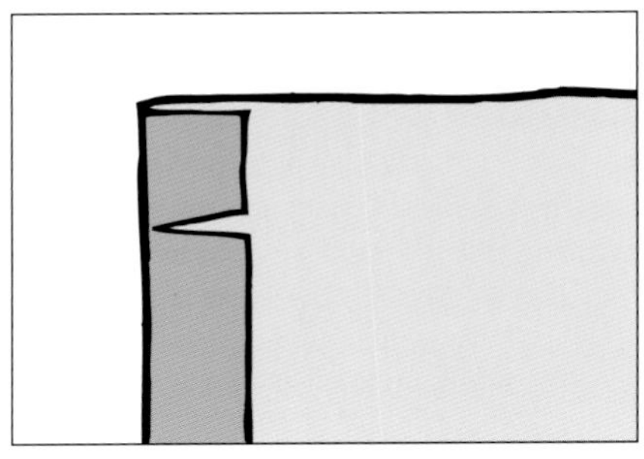

4 *Finally, hem the top of the curtain, snipping into the hem along both sides of the fold line to ease the material.*

Loose-lined curtains

Making the curtains

In these loose-lined curtains, the lining is attached to the front fabric at the top and sides only and so hangs loose, rather than the front and lining fabrics being sewn to each other as in conventional locked-in lined curtains. The easiest way to make loose-lined curtains is by the 'tube method', so called because a tube is made with the front and lining fabrics. These are the easiest type of lined curtain to make. (To make curtains with a locked-in lining, follow the instructions on pages 60–61.)

Join drops and press seams open on both the front and the lining fabrics (see pages 50–51). The lining fabric should be about 10cm (4in) narrower than the front fabric and 8cm (3¼in) shorter. Finish the bottom of the lining by machine stitching a double 5cm (2in) hem. Then lay the fabrics right sides together, with the bottom edge of the lining 18cm (7in) short of the bottom raw edge of the front fabric. Machine stitch the sides of the curtain, taking a 1.5cm (⅝in) seam allowance, with the edges of the lining and front fabric aligned, stopping well short of the top and bottom to allow for mitring.

You now have a tube of fabric. Turn it right side out and press the sides so that the front fabric comes round to the back an equal amount at each edge. One way of doing this is to mark the middle of the wrong side of both the front fabric and the lining with tailor's chalk, then match the marks when pressing the edges. Make a double 8cm (3¼in) hem on the front fabric, which will sit behind and just be covered by the lining, sewing in leadweight tape or weights, and finish the corners with mitres (see page 57). Alternatively, if you are a perfectionist or there is any doubt about the pole, track or floor being exactly level, tack the hem and hang the curtains. After several days, make any necessary adjustments to the hem and finish with slip stitching.

To finish the top of the curtain, measure up the finished length from the hem and mark the line with pins. Turn down the front fabric along this line. If necessary, trim back any excess front fabric and trim the lining so that it fits neatly underneath it. Turn in the sides of the turnback (see page 57) and attach the heading tape (see pages 52–53). Gather the heading to the required length and neatly tie up the loose strings. Finally, hang the curtains.

If the curtain is designed to hang straight, fix the folds by a process known as 'dressing' or 'draping' the curtain. To do this, pull the curtain closed and arrange the fabric into folds. Do this by tugging the hem in line with the pleats at the top of the curtain, and then running your fingers down the length of the curtain to create full-length pleats. Keeping these in place, carefully draw the curtain back. Using tape or strips of scrap fabric, gently tie the curtain in several places

▲ *These luxurious, heavy curtains are fixed at the top, but are looped back during the day to reveal their contrasting lime-green lining. Coloured lining can be made in any fabric, plain or patterned, so long as it has sufficient body to support the front fabric and is colourfast in sunlight.*

▶ *The plain lining of these striped curtains has been extended round to the front, to make a contrasting edging along the top and down the sides. Each curtain is hung from its own iron rod, and the rods are placed at different heights on the wall, which cleverly allows a considerable draught-excluding overlap.*

Lined curtains

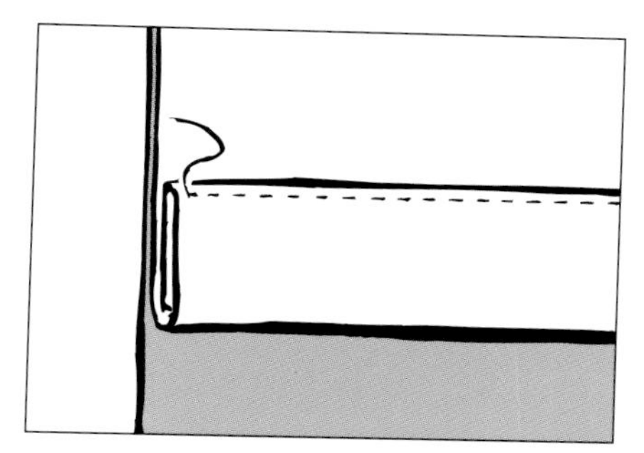

1 Machine stitch a double hem on the lining then place it on the main fabric, 18cm (7in) up from the bottom.

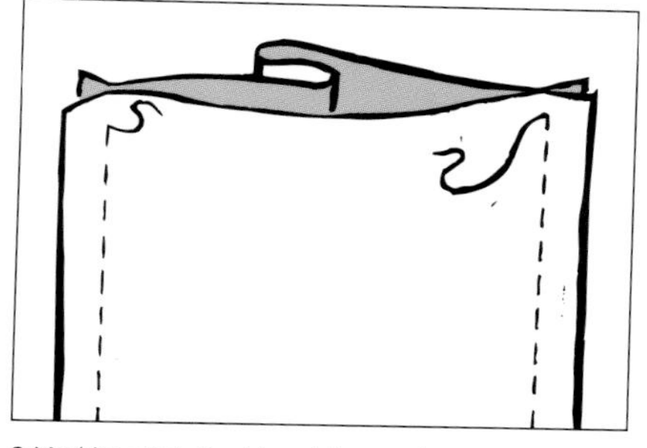

2 Machine stitch the sides of the curtain, stopping short of the top and bottom to leave room for mitring.

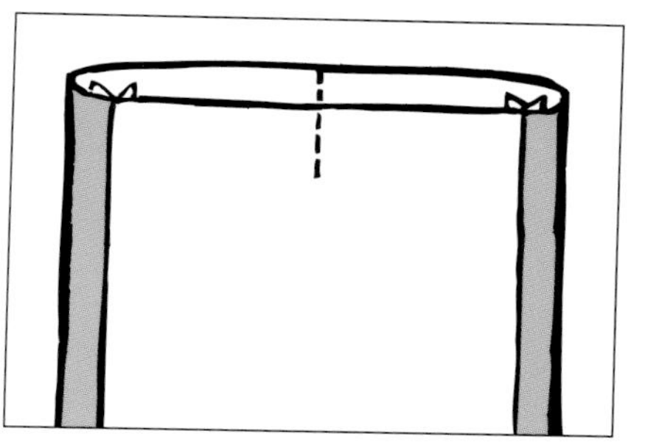

3 Turn the fabric tube right side out, and press the sides, matching the centre points of both fabrics.

up its length, starting near the bottom. Leave it for as long as possible, a few days at the least, to ensure the folds are fixed.

Detachable linings

Detachable linings can be removed in summer or for cleaning. Make up the front fabric and the lining as for two separate unlined curtains (see page 57). The lining does not need to be so fully gathered as the front curtain. Sew the top of the lining into special tape designed for the top of detachable linings. Shaped in profile like an upside-down 'Y', the raw top edge of the lining fabric is inserted within the open bottom section of the tape and sewn along its bottom. Curtain hooks are then looped through the top of this tape, before being hooked through the heading tape at the top of the front curtain fabric, and into rings or runners on the pole or track.

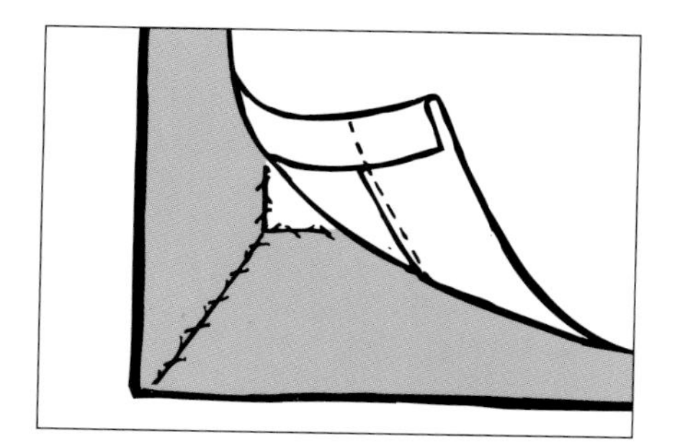

4 Unfold the hem and refold the hem and side seam into a mitre. Slip stitch the diagonal join and the hem.

5 Close the curtain and use your hands to arrange the folds. Tie them in place and leave for a few days.

Detachable linings

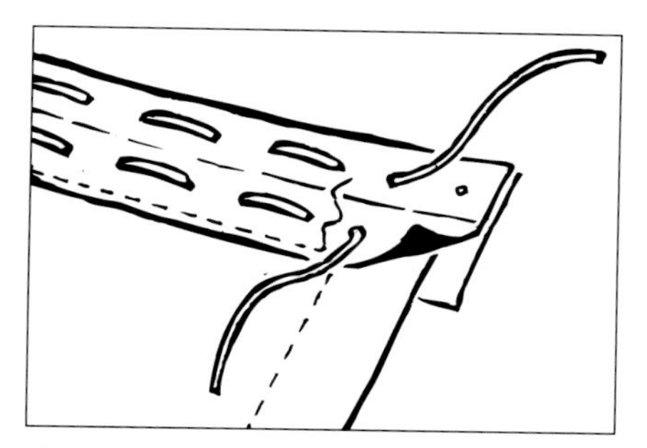

Place the edge of the lining between the two halves of the lining tape, overlapping and turning under the ends.

Locked-in lined curtains

▲ *Lining and interlining sewn into curtains give the front fabric greater body so that it hangs in handsome folds, as seen in these boldly checked silk curtains. The additional layers also help to exclude sound, light and draughts when the curtains are drawn closed.*

Locked-in lined curtains

Locked-in lined curtains take a little more time and more hand stitching than loose-lined curtains, but the result is worth it. Once you have mastered this technique, an option is to add a layer of interlining between the lining and the main fabric (see opposite).

Buy the front fabric and the lining in the same widths if possible. Cut all the lengths and join the seams of the front and lining as usual (see pages 50–51). Cut the lining 8cm (3¼in) narrower than the front fabric and 8cm (3¼in) shorter.

Making the curtains

On the main fabric, fold over and press a 4cm (1½in) turning at both sides and a double 8cm (3¼in) hem, mitring the corners and inserting weights as you go (see page 57). Herringbone stitch the side turns and slip stitch the hem.

You are now ready to attach the lining. Machine stitch a double 5cm (2in) hem along the bottom of the lining, then lay it in place on the curtain, wrong sides together. Check that the lining is centred on the curtain, and about 2cm (¾in) from the bottom. Fold the lining back on itself so that there is a fold formed along the centre. Use lock stitch to attach the lining to the front fabric along the line of this fold. Sew from the top to the bottom edge, making a stitch every 10–15cm (4–6in). Pick up only a thread or two of the front fabric so that the lock

Locked-in lining

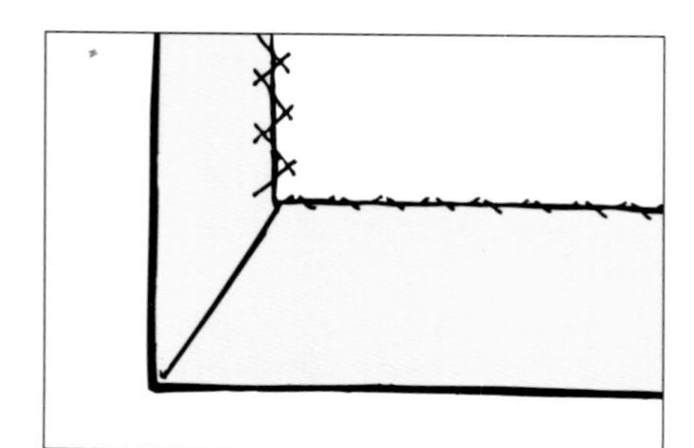

1 Turn back the side and bottom edges of the front fabric, mitring corners, and herringbone stitch in place.

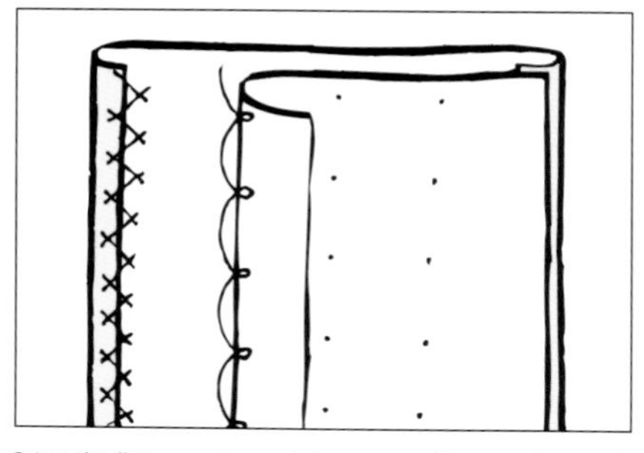

2 Lay the lining on the curtain, wrong sides together, and lock stitch to the front fabric down the centre.

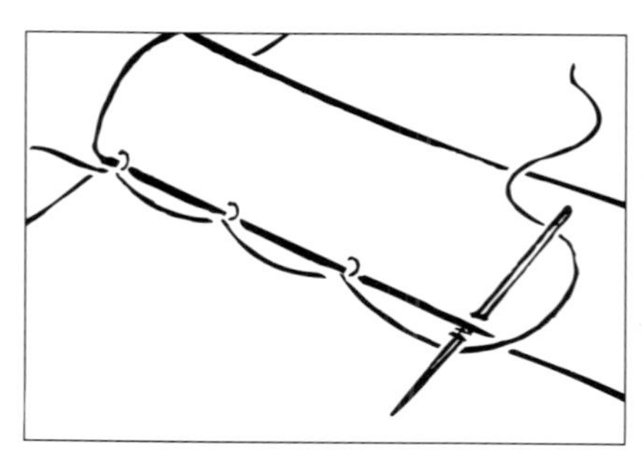

3 To lock stitch, pull up only a few threads from the main fabric so that the stitches do not show on the right side.

stitch will be invisible on the finished curtain. The sewing needs to be loose, without any tension, so use a single long thread for each row, rather than knotting together shorter lengths as you work. Use thread that matches the front fabric. Continue lock stitching along the widths and the half widths. Repeat for the other half of the curtain.

Turn under, press and slip stitch the edges of the lining to the turnback of the front fabric, so that equal amounts of front fabric show at each side. Slip stitch the bottom edge of the lining to the front fabric, unless the front fabric hem is tacked for final adjustment after the curtains are hung. In this case do not sew the bottom edge of the lining until the front fabric hem has been sewn.

When the lining is attached, complete the heading by turning back the front fabric and sewing the heading tape over the raw edge in the usual way (see pages 52–53). You can now gather up the curtain, hang it and dress the folds (see pages 58–59).

Interlined curtains

Interlined curtains undoubtedly look smarter than any other type of curtain. Not only is their appearance magnificent, but their bulk and weight make them extremely efficient excluders of draughts and light. They are also heavy and so should be hung only from the strongest, well-fixed track or pole.

Making interlined curtains is a big job, requiring concentration and immense patience.

▲ *Lining needs to be made from a sturdy fabric to support the front fabric, especially when the curtains are made from heavy woollen twill. The weight of these curtains is increased by the pleats, so it is essential that the rods from which they hang are securely fixed above the window.*

You need plenty of table space, plenty of time in which to work undisturbed and plenty of experience in curtain making. The difficulty is in keeping everything flat and straight so that the curtains hang straight and smooth at the end. Padded weights help, and some people also use large bulldog clips.

Making the curtains

Joins in the interlining need flat seams, made by overlapping the material by 2cm (¾in) and zigzag stitching over the cut edges. Cut the interlining to the exact size of the finished curtain (i.e. smaller than the main curtain fabric, which will have hem allowances). Fold in the side turns and hem allowance on the curtain fabric and press, then unfold them and place the interlining inside the creases.

Attach the interlining to the main fabric with lock stitch, as for the lining, but when you complete each row, lock stitch the bottom edge of the interlining along the hemline, from the last vertical row of lock stitch to the one you have just completed. Now fold and sew the turnbacks down each side of the curtain with herringbone stitch. Trim the hem allowance down to 10cm (4in), then herringbone stitch this to the interlining. Attach the lining as before.

Hems and edges can be padded for a more substantial look. Cut the interlining wider and deeper than the finished curtain. Turn back the edges and hem of the interlining, first lock stitching the lines of these folds to the edge and hem creases on the front fabric.

Interlined curtains

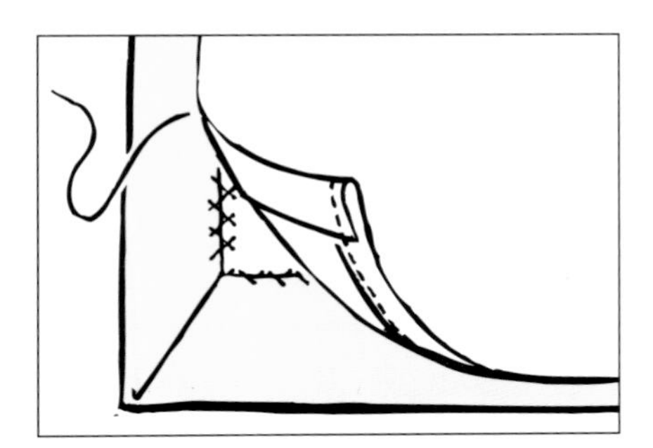

4 Turn under the edges of the lining and slip stitch to the turnings of the curtain, around three sides.

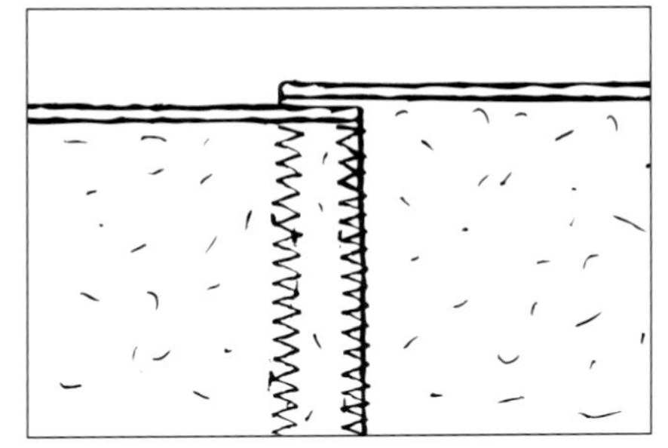

1 Join widths of interlining by overlapping them and machine zigzagging over the cut edges.

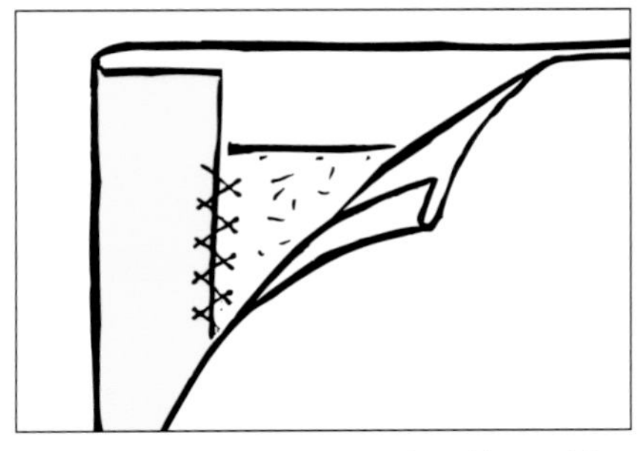

2 Interlining is inserted between the front fabric and the lining, and attached to the front fabric with lock stitch.

Pelmets, valances, swags and tails

▲ *This shaped pelmet with a zigzag bottom edge makes a dramatic impact when the curtains are open and the points are outlined against daylight. Covered in the same fabric as the curtains, the pelmet is deep enough not to look skimpy, and is well proportioned in relation to the size of the window and the length of the curtains.*

The space above curtains offers plenty of scope for decorative interest. If you decide against having a pole, then a world of pelmets, valances and other ornamental toppings, such as swags and tails, opens up. All manner of designs and fabrics are possible.

Pelmets

A pelmet can be made of stiffened fabric or plain wood, fixed onto a board, or shelf, that is then fixed to the wall. The simplest fabric-covered pelmet is rectangular when looked at face-on, and covered with the same fabric as the curtains. More exciting alternatives might have a shaped lower edge, such as scallops, zigzags or castellations. Some pelmets have a shaped upper edge too. A pelmet can be decorated with trimmings such as ribbon, braid, tassels or fringing, while a large window can be made grand with a pelmet formed from magnificent swags and tails.

Using a different fabric from the curtain material for a heading can make an attractive contrast and is an opportunity to use a more expensive fabric than you could afford for the curtains themselves. It could have similar colours but a bolder pattern, perhaps, or a pattern that will be shown off to greater effect when flat on the pelmet rather than lost in curtain folds. Checks give definition to striped curtains, while stripes give a refreshing finish to floral cotton curtains. Alternatively, use a plain fabric with a contrasting edging, or create your own fabric design, using appliqué, embroidery or paints.

Pelmets

1 A pelmet board is fixed above the window so that the pelmet will eventually conceal the curtain heading.

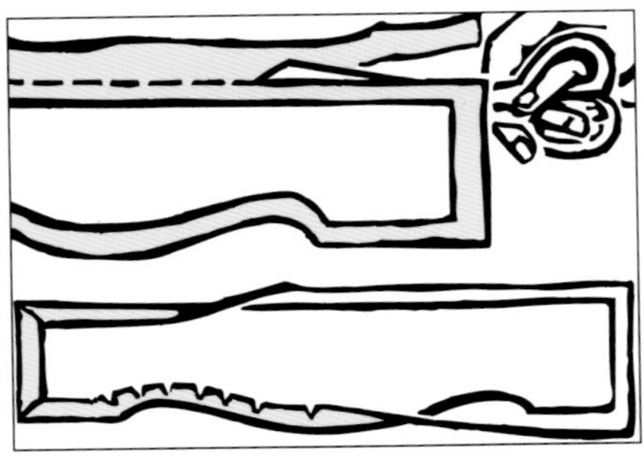

2 Fabric is attached to the stiffened pelmet shape and the edges are turned over to the wrong side.

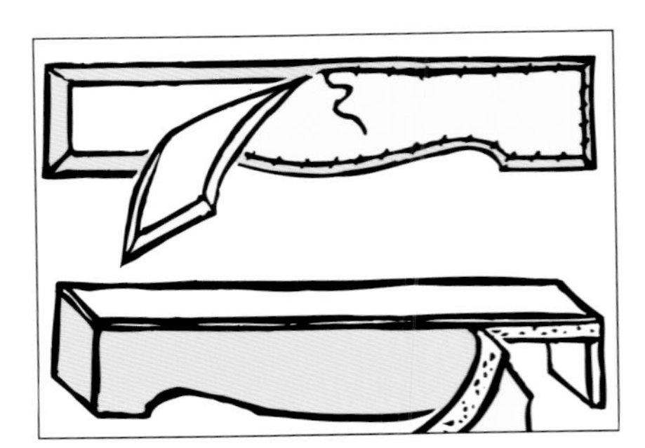

3 Lining is slip stitched to the back, then the pelmet fixed round three sides of the board with Velcro fastener.

Valance creator

1 Feed fabric through the spiral hooks from back to front, pull into a loop and secure the tail behind.

2 The finished ruffles hide the supporting hooks, and the whole result gives a 'swag and tail' effect.

A wooden pelmet can be made from solid wood, plywood, or MDF (medium-density fibreboard), which is easier to saw into interesting shapes than timber. It can be painted, or it can be decorated with glued objects around the edges or in patterns: shells, rope or beads, for example.

Making a pelmet

Cut a 10cm (4in)-deep pelmet board from 12mm (½in)-thick plywood, making it the length of the curtain track plus about 12cm (5in) to give 6cm (2½in) clearance at each end. Glue and screw end pieces to form returns, if desired. Fix the pelmet board to the wall just above the window and track using angle brackets fixed at 20cm (8in) intervals, making sure it will conceal the curtain heading.

Cut out the pelmet shape from stiffening material, making it long enough to fit around the sides and front of the pelmet board. The traditional stiffener is buckram, which is sewn in place with interlining. Iron-on buckram is also available. PVC self-adhesive stiffener can also be used, and makes the job a lot easier. It has graph backing paper, enabling you to cut your own designs easily, and several printed designs that can be followed. The single-sided type of self-adhesive stiffener, which has a peel-off strip on one side and integral velour backing which acts as both lining and Velcro on the other, requires no lining; but the double-sided type, which sticks to both front fabric and lining to give a neater finish, does.

Cut out the same shape from the main fabric, adding 3cm (1¼in) for a turning all round. Attach the stiffener to the wrong side of the fabric. Turn the fabric edges over, clipping into the curves and corners so that the fabric lies flat. Cut lining fabric 1.5cm (⅝in) larger all round than the pelmet shape. Turn and press this allowance under and attach the lining to the back of the pelmet, slip stitching it to the main fabric. Attach the pelmet to the top edge of the board using Velcro – where necessary stapling or tacking the hooked half to the board and the soft half to the back of the pelmet.

▲ Unsewn fabric, draped in an elegant curve across the top of this narrow window and finished with a puff at each corner, makes a charming unstructured swag. Such an effect is easy to achieve with a valance creator and is an appealing alternative to the tortured folds of some more sophisticated window headings.

Swags and tails

Hung from a pelmet board, swags and tails create an illusion of continuous drapery. Made up in many forms, swags and tails range in complexity from one swag to many and from pleated ones cut from several pieces of fabric to gathered ones made from a single piece of cloth. Swags and tails are best suited to full-length curtains on large windows.

Lambrequins

A lambrequin is the name given to a flat fabric shape which frames the window. Usually hanging down at the sides, it can front a blind or simple net or lace curtain, or it can stand alone at a window where no curtain is necessary.

Valances

In addition to being made into pelmets and lambrequins, fabric can be gathered or sculpted into folds or pleats, making a type of short fixed curtain known as a valance. An attached valance is a decorative fold of fabric which hangs down from the top of the actual curtain, giving you the best of both worlds as you have a handsome curtain top and you can hang the curtains from a pole.

Fabric can also be draped across the top of the window, with or without curtains or a blind. It should be lined to give it body and support, and can then be arranged over and fixed to a pole or rod (separate from the curtain pole if there is one), wooden or metal curtain hold-backs or some other prop.

A valance creator is a curly-ended bracket around which fabric can be wrapped. It is fixed to the wall above and to each side of the window. Feed the fabric through from the back of the spiral to the front, in a loop, with the tail secured to the back, hanging down. The loops of fabric, creating gathers, hide the brackets of the valance creator.

Tie-backs and hold-backs

▶ *A pair of original and amusing fabric tie-backs have been created by taking conventional curtain restraints and sewing mother-of-pearl buttons all over them. These twinkle in the light from the window, echoing the spots of glitter on the curtains themselves.*

During the day, curtains are drawn back to let as much light as possible into a room or to reveal other layers of curtain dressing such as lace, net or a light-diffusing blind. The curtains either hang straight down or can be restrained by tie-backs or hold-backs fixed to the wall at the sides of the window. Tie-backs are made of fabric, rope, cord or any other soft material that can be tied, and hold-backs are made of metal or wood.

A tie-back can be decorated with anything that can be sewn or glued to a suitable backing, threaded onto cord or plaited into a rope, and which is sufficiently resilient to withstand the daily business of being undone and done up again. Beads, for instance, can be sewn or threaded; a fringe of corks can be threaded together; roses and leaves made from brilliantly coloured velvet or glazed cotton can look stunning; a plait of hessian rope looks rugged and is well suited to fabrics such as unbleached calico or natural linen.

Fabric tie-backs

A fabric tie-back consists of two shaped pieces of material sewn together with a layer of buckram or other stiffener sandwiched in between. This is fastened to a hook or loop on the wall by means of brass rings or ties sewn into each end. The fabric could be the same as the curtain or the pelmet, or of another design entirely. Edges of tie-backs can be defined by binding them with a contrast fabric, known as bound-edge binding, edging them with braid or inserting piping.

Making a fabric tie-back

To make a fabric tie-back, first loop a flexible tape measure around a curtain, drawn open, and hold the ends next to the wall where it will be fixed to find the length. Decide how wide it is to be. Make a rectangular paper pattern to the length and depth you want. Fold this in half along the length and if you want the ends to be rounded or curved, draw these in on one half. Cut through both thicknesses of paper around your shape and unfold the pattern. Pin it around the curtain to check it is the right size, and make any adjustments as necessary.

Use the pattern to cut out four pieces of fabric (two for each tie-back), adding 1.5cm (⅝in) all round for seam allowances. For each tie-back also cut out a piece of stiffener without the seam allowance. Attach one

Tie-backs

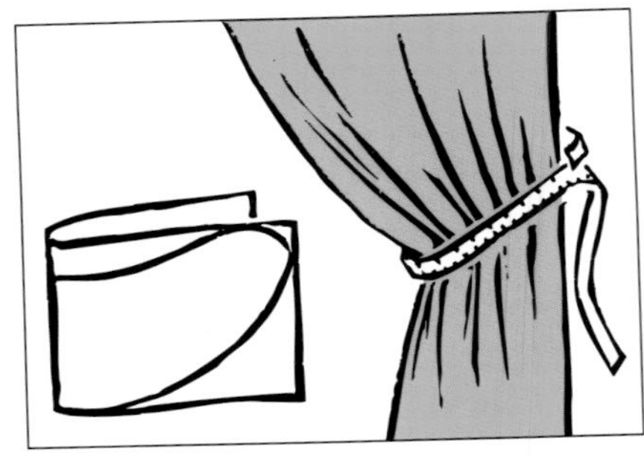

1 Use a tape measure to calculate the dimensions of the tie-back, then make a paper pattern of the exact shape.

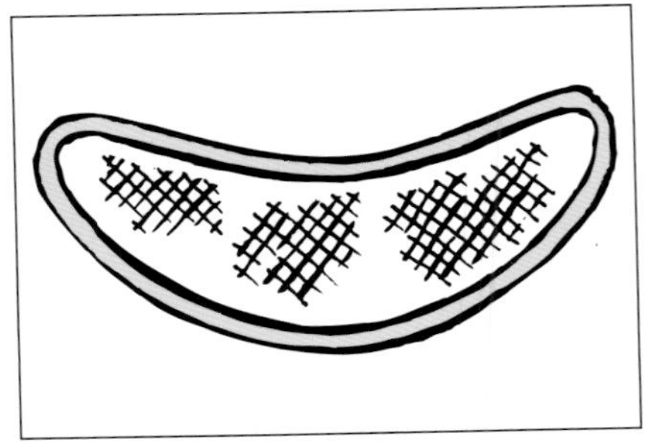

2 Cut two pieces of stiffener and four pieces of fabric, adding a seam allowance. Iron on the stiffener.

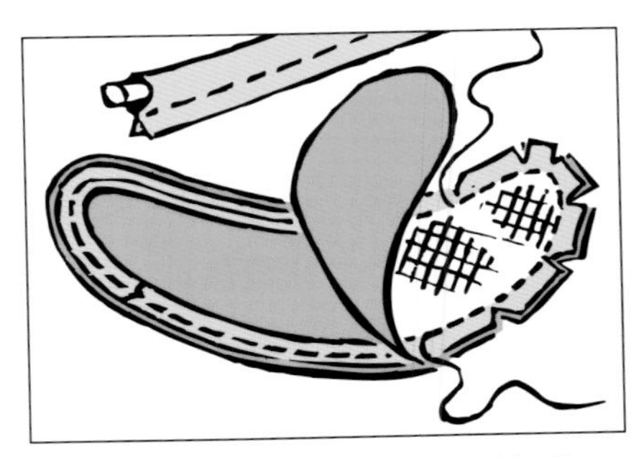

3 Stitch on piping, if used, then both pieces, right sides together, leaving an opening for turning.

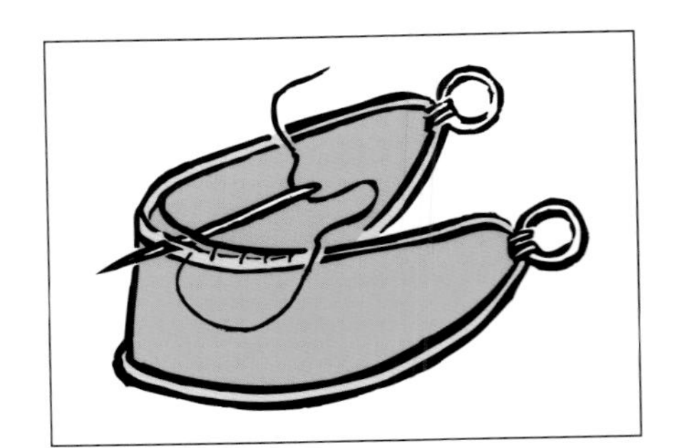

4 Turn right side out, slip stitch closed, then sew on rings at each end, or in far enough so that they are hidden.

piece of stiffener in the centre of the wrong side of one piece of fabric. The simplest to use is iron-on stiffener.

Place the fabric pieces right sides together and machine stitch along the seam line, leaving an opening to turn the tie-back through. Trim the edges, clip the curves or corners and turn the tie-back right side out. Press flat.

Turn in the open edges and slip stitch the gap closed. Rings can be sewn at each end, or further in so that they are hidden when the tie-back is in use.

Piping on a tie-back

Piping is made by enclosing piping cord in a strip of fabric cut on the bias. The length of fabric strip must allow for piping to go right round the shape, plus an extra 3cm (1¼in) for overlapping the ends. You may find it necessary to join strips in order to achieve the right length. The width of the fabric strip needs to be the circumference of the piping cord plus 3cm (1¼in), i.e. twice the seam allowance. The strip of fabric is folded in half and the cord enclosed within it. The cord should be stitched in as close to the fold as possible, and the raw edges of the seam allowance left.

If using piping on a tie-back, attach it at the point of sewing the two main fabric pieces together. It is stitched to the right side of the fabric at the seam line. To do this, align the raw edges of the tie-back sections and the piping. When the piping turns a corner, a section will need to be clipped out of the seam allowance at that point to ensure the fabric does not kink.

To finish off, turn the tie-back the right way out and sew up the gap with slip stitch, on the inside edge of the piping.

Bound edges on a tie-back

You can use ready-made bias binding, but to get just the binding you want, cut strips of contrasting fabric on the bias. Binding strips need to be twice the finished depth required, plus 3cm (1¼in) for seam allowances.

When making bound edges, cut out the fabric pieces for the tie-back to the required size and attach the stiffener, as previously, to the wrong side of one piece. This time, place the wrong sides of the tie-back pieces together and machine stitch around the edge.

Fold over 1.5cm (⅝in) along each edge of the binding strip and press, then fold the strip in half lengthways and press again. Open out the last fold and align the raw edge of the binding with the raw edge of the tie-back, right sides together. Sew a 1.5cm (⅝in) seam. Bring the edging over the raw edges of the tie-back and slip stitch the seam on the reverse side along the stitch line, trimming the enclosed edges if necessary. Turn under at the ends to neaten them.

Hold-backs

Hold-backs made of wood are generally shaped something like a mushroom, with a base, a stalk and a round head decorated with carving or gilding, behind which the curtain is looped when drawn open. You can paint or stain a wooden hold-back to match or complement the curtain fabric or the finish of other surfaces in the room.

Metal hold-backs are either fixed or hinged. A fixed one curls out from the wall like an arm, embracing the curtain when it is drawn back behind it. It can look odd when the curtain is closed and it has nothing to hold. This problem can be overcome if the curtain hangs well out from the wall and hides it when drawn closed, without it creating a protuberance in the fabric.

A hinged, hook-shaped metal hold-back has a hinge or ring near the wall which allows it to hang down flat when it is not holding back the curtain. When the curtain is drawn open the hold-back is lifted up and the fullness of the curtain looped into it, so that it stands out from the wall.

▲ *Hold-backs are an ideal opportunity for extra decoration and unusual touches. This leaf in thin gilded metal dresses up the plainest of curtains made in inexpensive fabric. It is attached to a thick shank that is then fixed to the wall, providing space in which to fit the curtain so that the leaf can be seen to full advantage.*

Bound-edge tie-back

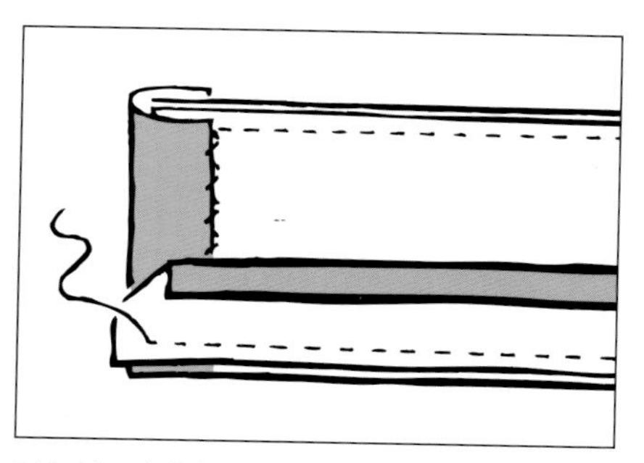

1 *Machine stitch the binding to the right side of the tie-back, raw edges aligning, with a 1.5cm (⅝in) seam.*

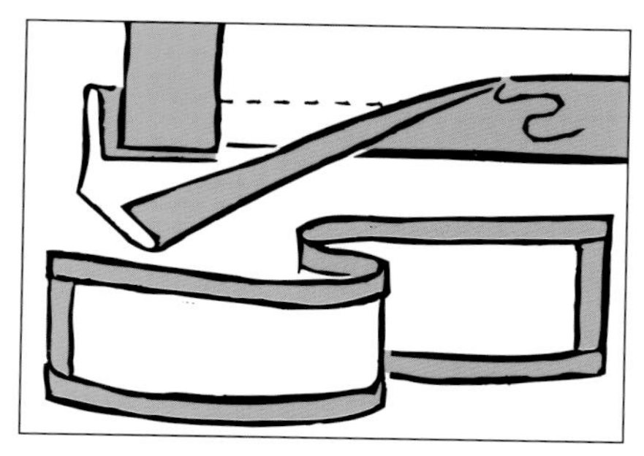

2 *Turn the binding over to the wrong side and slip stitch in place, turning under the ends where necessary.*

Blinds

For many windows in the home, blinds are the simple, stylish solution. Where a room is small and space is important, or where there is little room at the sides of a window, it may be far more appropriate to fit a flat roller or Roman blind neatly within the window frame than curtains from a raised track or pole. Flat blinds will show off fabric well; can be an inexpensive choice; and if sized correctly and lined, they can provide excellent insulation.

There are blinds to suit most practical and decorative requirements, ranging from the very basic to the flamboyant. They can be left unlined - the lighter fabrics useful for allowing light to pass through, but hiding an uninspiring view or giving privacy - or they can be lined to improve their light-blocking and insulating capabilities.

Depending on their design, blinds can be hung in almost any room or situation. Crooked windows in old houses are probably the one exception, because blinds do need to be hung absolutely straight and will look odd at a window out of true. For a window that is wider than it is long, two or more blinds fixed side by side work better than a single wide blind which may be too large to operate well.

The most basic of blinds is a piece of flat, lightweight fabric permanently fixed over a window to block out an unpleasant view but allow light into the room. A little more versatile than this, but still simple, is the tie blind, which should only be used where it will not need to be raised and lowered frequently – perhaps in a bathroom. It consists of a piece of unlined fabric to which are attached four ribbons or fabric strips. Fixed at the top of the blind, about a quarter of the width in from either edge, these hang down – two to the front and two to the back – and are tied together at each side under the blind's bottom edge. The drop of the blind is adjusted as required by re-tying the ties at different heights. The blind itself can be attached to a heading board using Velcro strip. A dowel can be sewn into the bottom hem to ensure the blind hangs with a straight bottom edge.

Roller blinds incorporate a sprung roller which facilitates the raising of the blind and takes up very little space above the window. They are useful for any situation where as much light as possible is required when the blind is up, but where they need to be pulled down frequently. They are also practical for windows that are set at an angle, such as in an attic conversion, as the batten at the bottom of the blind can be restrained beneath the window by cup hooks, while the blind itself follows the sloping line of the roof.

◀ *An unusual arrangement of translucent white roller blinds in a minimalist interior. One is set into the window rebate and pulls down, while the other larger blind pulls up from a box on the floor and covers the entire window, with a wide margin on each side.*

◀ *An impressively lofty kitchen-cum-dining room in a modern building has louvred blinds built into the windows, in keeping with the uncluttered interior. The great advantage of louvred blinds is that the amount of shade can be varied when the blind is let down, or the blind can be pulled up completely.*

▲ *Slatted wooden blinds like these, which roll up inside the pull-up string, can be used as inexpensive room dividers as well as shade and privacy providers. Here they conceal the kitchen in one corner of the sitting room, when let down. They are also a good choice to tone in with the cane furniture and wood-slat doors.*

▲ *A single huge blind for this large window space would be too cumbersome to pull up; instead, there are three elegant Roman blinds. The centre one is wider, conforming in size to the window behind, and made from the same green linen as the left-hand chair, while the others are white to match the right-hand chair.*

Roller blinds offer little in the way of insulation, however, although they will filter bright light and create privacy at night. Because they can be made of spongeable fabric, they are useful in frequently damp rooms such as kitchens and bathrooms. Specially stiffened fabric is readily available for making roller blinds, but ordinary fabrics (except very loosely woven ones) can be used as long as they are sprayed with, or dipped into, a stiffener before being made up.

The Roman blind is the smartest, most regimented of blinds. When pulled up, it folds away neatly in pleats tucked behind each other. The regularity and crispness of these pleats is created by narrow strips of wood, usually lath or dowelling, slotted into a series of horizontal fabric pockets on the back of the blind and creating ridges. When the blind is pulled up by the cords, which run through small brass or plastic rings that are sewn to the edge of each pocket, the ridges are hoisted up to fold the blind into its neat pleats. Many people prefer the appearance of Roman blinds to curtains because, while they look equally luxurious (especially if padded with lightweight interlining), they are unfussy.

When drawn up, a Roman blind blocks out more light than a roller blind does, but if it is lined (and possibly lightly interlined) it is as good as a curtain for excluding draughts and light, especially if it fits the window well or hangs so that the edges overlap the architrave or reveal. Because of the reinforced folds stacking up at the back of it when drawn up, the Roman blind requires a certain depth of window in which to operate.

Gathered blinds: Austrian, pull-up and festoon

Quite different from the simple appearance of flat blinds are the various types of gathered blinds which all involve festoons of fabric, some also ruched. The more extravagant of these are suited to a certain type of heavily decorated interior rather than anywhere requiring a fresh, contemporary feel, especially in a small room.

The Austrian blind is pulled up by means of cords and rings like a Roman blind but has a gathered or pleated heading which bunches up into a series of puffs or swags, and does not have the strips of dowelling to form strict pleats. Like the Roman blind, it can provide good draft and light exclusion. In certain situations – in simply furnished rooms with tall ceilings and windows, for example – it can be used successfully if care is taken to avoid making a place feel claustrophobic. This is especially true if the blind looks like a curtain when let down, falling straight to the floor (or window sill) with no ruches at the bottom. Some people call this type of blind a 'pull-up curtain'.

Similar to an Austrian blind, a festoon blind retains the swags down its entire length when let down. A further variation is known as a tailed Austrian blind, which by omitting cords at the edges of the blind allows the sides to trail and flop down.

▲ *A series of loosely hanging, narrow Roman blinds, made from natural textured linen, make a strong and witty impact on this series of folding glass-topped doors. Each blind is knotted at the bottom and covers a pane of glass, emphasizing the door's shape and the number of panels.*

Fabrics and finishes

Fabrics for blinds need to be chosen with some care. Because an Austrian blind makes an impact through its puffed-up fullness, it should be made with a plain fabric or one with an unfussy pattern, such as stripes.

The simplicity of the roller blind and the regimented form of the Roman blind also call for fabrics which are plain, either with an interesting texture or patterned in a graphic style. Before deciding on a particular fabric, imagine, for instance, how a Roman blind would look once pulled up into its pleats. Alternatively, picture fabric is fun on a roller blind in a bathroom or kitchen, and fresh patterns like stripes and checks look good on any type of blind. Flat blinds are better for large patterns than ones with lots of folds.

The fabric used for making any type of blind must be cut absolutely straight or it will look shoddy once it is finished and hung. If there is any sort of pattern on the fabric, make sure it is arranged symmetrically across the blind. It must also be printed true. Examine your chosen fabric carefully before starting to make the blind, and if it is faulty in this or any other respect, return it immediately to the shop.

Interest and definition can be added to a blind with a band of contrasting fabric or trimming set back from the edges. If this trimming is to be continued across the bottom of a Roman blind, the last flap of fabric has to be made extra deep so that the bottom border is not hidden when the blind is pulled up.

A roller blind can be made more interesting if it has a shaped bottom edge, coming down at an angle, for example, or cut in a pattern of points or castellations. The shaped part hangs below the bottom batten, and the string should be attached to the batten rather than the shape below it.

Non-fabric blinds

Blinds do not, of course, have to be made of fabric. They can be constructed from cane, bamboo, wooden slats, paper and even metal, and are widely available in many styles, designs and colours (see pages 76–77).

First steps to making blinds

▶ *A neat and restrained use of a Roman blind. This one is tucked inside the architrave of the window and is made from plain white linen which allows sunlight to glow through it, making it appear almost luminous, as well as matching the pure white paint on the window and the restrained pattern of the walls.*

Measuring up for blinds

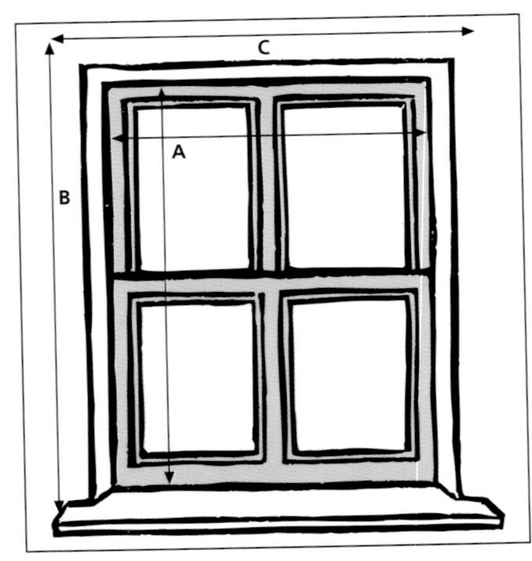

Measure the height and width of the window, either inside the recess or to cover the architrave.

Measuring up and estimating quantities

Decide exactly where the blind is to hang, then measure up, as follows, to find the finished dimensions and the amount of fabric you will need for your blind.

For a recessed blind, measure the height and width of the recess (A). For roller blind fabric, deduct 3cm (1¼in) from the width to account for the ends of the mechanism within the window frame.

For a face-fixed blind, measure from the top of the hanging system at the chosen height to the sill for the drop (B) (or past the sill for a longer blind), and for the width add 5cm (2in) either side of the recess (C) so that the light will be blocked out. Get extra fabric if you plan to wrap the hanging batten with the same fabric in order to disguise it.

Roman blind construction

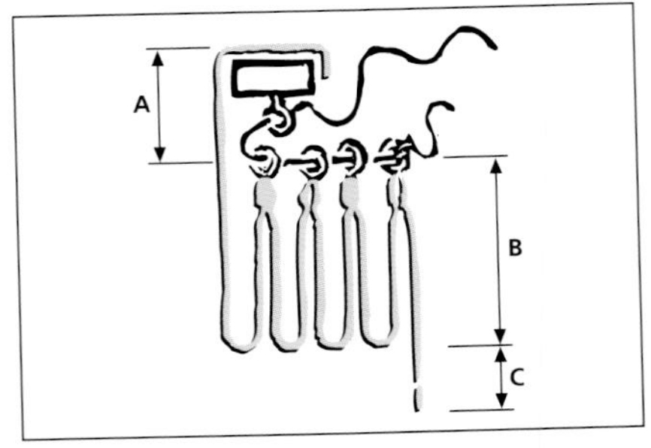

A fully pulled-up Roman blind. A = hanging allowance; B = depth of pleats; C = lower flap.

Roller blind

For a roller blind add an extra 30cm (12in) to the length for a hem at the bottom and to cover the roller at the top.

Austrian blind or pull-up curtain

For an Austrian blind allow an extra 5cm (2in) for the turnback at the top and 20cm (8in) for a double hem at the bottom. The width of fabric you need is two and a half times the length of the heading batten plus 4cm (1½in) for turnbacks at the sides. If you are lining the blind, you will need roughly the same amount of lining fabric.

To achieve the curtain effect when the blind is down, make the blind's finished length equal to the distance from the window top to the sill. However, if you want to retain the ruched look at the bottom when the blind is down, make it about 45cm (18in) longer.

Roman blind

Estimating quantities for a Roman blind needs careful working out so make sure you check your calculation. Make a clearly drawn sketch and mark all the measurements on it so that you can refer to them when making up the blind. When measuring up, allow an extra 6cm (2¼in) for the hem and ridge pocket at the bottom and 6cm (2¼in) to wrap over a 5 x 2.5cm (2 x 1in) heading or fixing batten at the top. You will also need to allow 6cm (2¼in) for a 3cm (1¼in) turnback at each side.

For the lining allow an extra 6cm (2¼in) for each ridge pocket for laths about 25 x 5mm (1 x ¼in), and cut it to the same width

Tools and equipment

To make a blind you will need the following materials and equipment. If you are sewing a Roman blind (see pages 72–73) or an Austrian blind (see pages 74–75), you will also need almost all the materials and equipment required for sewing curtains (see page 49) to create the fabric part of the blind. Roman and Austrian blinds are suspended from a batten, approximately 5 x 2.5cm (2 x 1in) by the width of the blind, which is fixed to the wall with screws and plugs as necessary and can be painted to match the decor or the fabric.

For measuring up and fixing

- Long wooden measure and a set square or T-square: to ensure that marking-up lines are perpendicular to the edges.
- Spirit level, a drill, screws and wall plugs, a hammer and tacks or staple gun and staples: for fixing the blind to the wall.
- Saw: for cutting the roller to size.
- Hammer: for the fitting.

For a roller blind

- A roller blind kit: consisting of a roller with spring, brackets, end cap and pin, wooden lath, cord holder and acorn (or these items bought separately).
- Pencil and masking tape.
- Liquid or spray stiffener: for untreated fabric.

For Roman and Austrian blinds/ pull-up curtains

- Cord, drop weight and wall cleat: for pulling up and lowering the blind.
- Brass or plastic rings: through which to thread the cord on the back of the blind.
- Screw-in eyelets, as many as there are cords at the back of the blind, plus one through which all cords go.
- Sewing machine with zip foot.
- 6, 10 or 12mm (¼, ⅜ or ½in) dowelling or lath, maximum 25 x 5mm (1 x ¼in): enough for all the pocket ridges in the blind (Roman).
- Velcro-backed heading tape or pencil pleat heading tape (Austrian).
- Leadweight tape (optional) (Austrian).
- Fringe or edging material (optional) (Austrian).

◄ *A carefully orchestrated scheme of white and washed-out blues, distressed plaster, metal and wood called for an understated window treatment: Austrian blinds in their simplest form, unadorned by fringes or other trimmings, in a crisply striped fabric.*

as the front fabric. For wood of different dimensions or dowelling, calculate the amount of fabric needed for each ridge pocket, adding a little extra so that the wood slides in easily.

To work out how many ridges you need, first decide how deep the piece of fabric at the top of the blind will be. This will usually extend above the last pleat by about 4–10cm (1½–4in) and will cover the eyelets and give room for the pleats to lie evenly. The deeper this hanging allowance, the more light is cut out when the blind is pulled up.

Also decide if the lower flap at the bottom of the blind will hang down below the rest of the pleats when the blind is closed to allow the bottom edge of the border, if you have one, to show. Subtract the hanging allowance and the bottom border allowance (if any) from the blind's finished length to give the folding length.

Decide how many pleats would be right for the proportions of the blind. A pleat is usually 20–30cm (8–12in) deep. To check that your imagined pleats fall within this range, and to establish their actual measurement, divide the blind's folding length by the number of pleats you want, plus an additional half-pleat. A full pleat is the complete fold of fabric between two ridges. The extra half-pleat is taken up by the fabric that falls from the last ridge to the bottom edge of the gathered-up pleats.

Having established the number and depth of pleats, you have finally arrived at the number of ridges and ridge pockets you need, which will, in turn, enable you to calculate the length of lining fabric you need.

Roman blinds

▶ *Blinds on the ceiling of a conservatory, as well as at the windows, help to prevent the room overheating in the strong mid-afternoon sun. In winter, the blinds can be completely folded back to allow maximum light to stream into the area.*

Making a Roman blind

Prepare the heading board using a length of wooden batten 5 x 2.5cm (2 x 1in), and as long as the blind's width. Paint it the same colour as the wall or window, or wrap it (ends included) in a piece of the front or lining fabric of the blind. Make any other necessary preparations, such as preparing screw holes with a bradawl, for fixing the batten in place after the blind has been attached to it.

Cut out the fabric and lining to the required sizes (see pages 70–71). Cut the fabric on a straight grain by drawing out a weft thread (going across the width of the fabric) and cutting along this line at the top and bottom of both front and lining fabrics.

Make sure you can easily see and read the sketch of the blind, with all measurements marked on it, which you made when measuring up (see pages 70–71). Refer to your drawing for measurements when taking all the following steps. Mark up the front fabric and the lining, using a right angle or set square to ensure the lines are perpendicular to the edges of the fabric. On the wrong side of the front fabric, draw the top edge of the blind (the drop line) 6cm (2¼in) from the top, the position of all the ridges down the blind, and the bottom edge of the finished blind. On the right side of the lining, mark the position and depth of each ridge.

Turn back the sides of the front fabric 3cm (1¼in) and press. Turn back the sides of the lining 4cm (1½in) and press. On the lining, sew the ridge pockets in place. Pin and tack every seam with great care before sewing, making sure they are exactly horizontal, as it is extremely important that these are straight; if they are not, the blinds will not hang or move up and down properly.

Lay the front fabric face down and the lining face up, centrally, on top of the front fabric. Match the pockets on the lining to the lines marking their position on the front fabric. Fold the pockets down, pin, tack, then stitch the lining to the front fabric, just above and very near the pocket stitching, using the zip foot attachment on your sewing machine.

Stitch the top edges of the fabric and lining together with a zigzag stitch. Slip stitch the lining to the front fabric down the sides, leaving the pockets free, and stopping 2 cm (¾in) from the bottom edge of the front fabric. Trim the lining to this level. Turn up and press the front fabric 2cm (¾in) from the bottom. Then turn it up again so that the line you drew previously to mark the bottom edge of the finished blind is along the fold. You should have a hem of about 4cm (1½in), which will form the pocket for the bottom ridge. If the hem is much too deep, turn back more at the bottom edge of the fabric. Sew across the hem, near to the fold, either with the machine or, if you prefer the stitches not to show on the front of the blind, slip stitch by hand.

The pieces of wood that will form the ridges (laths) now have to be cut to size. The bottom one needs to be slightly shorter than the width of the finished blind, the others slightly shorter than the width of the lining. Insert these into their pockets and slip stitch the ends closed.

Sew the rings to the ridges (except the bottom edge ridge) in vertical rows spread evenly across the back of the blind at intervals of about 30–60cm (1–2ft), depending on the width of the blind. The first and last rows should be about 8cm (3¼in) in from the edges of the blind. Cut the cord and tie a piece to each bottom ring, threading it up through the other rings in each row.

At the top of the blind, lay the hanging batten on the blind so that the drop line is along what will be the top front edge of the batten when it is fixed to the window or wall. Wrap the blind tightly around to the back of the batten, tacking and stapling along the back to attach it securely. Alternatively, if the weight of the fabric you are using can be borne, the blind can be fixed to the hanging batten by using Velcro or strong double-sided tape.

Screw in the eyelets for the cords to go through before they drop, each eyelet corresponding to each row of rings on the back of the blind, with one extra in line with these near the end of the batten. Thread the cords up through the eyelets and along to one side.

Making a Roman blind

1 *Cut out main fabric and lining to size, plus allowances, and divide up into equal sections for the pleats.*

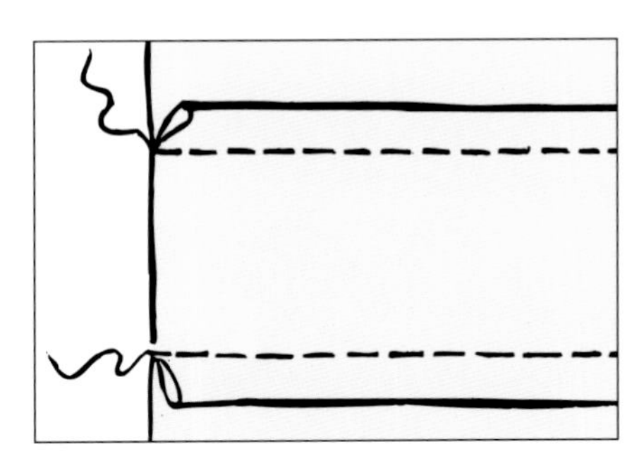

2 *On the lining, match pairs of lines for the ridges, wrong sides together, and stitch along the lines to form casings.*

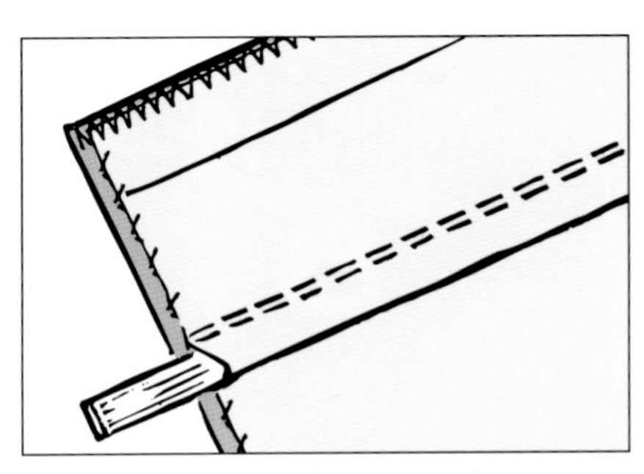

3 *Position the lining centrally on the main fabric and stitch the two together as described. Then insert laths.*

4 *Trim off lining at the bottom edge and turn up main fabric to form casing and sew rings on. Insert the batten.*

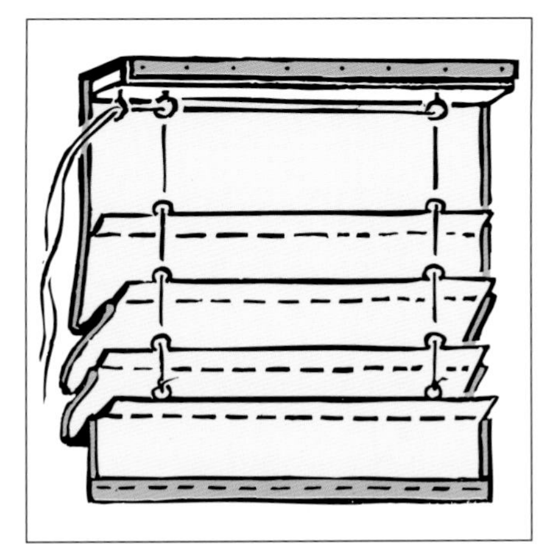

5 *Fix blind to heading board. Attach screw eyes and thread up cord from bottom to top. Fix to the window.*

Fix the heading batten to the window or to the wall using small brackets or fix it directly up into the recess of the window, then fit the cord cleat to the wall. The cleat needs careful positioning: if it is too far forward the cords will catch on the blind and spoil it. Finally, thread the cords through the drop weight, cut them to the same length and knot them.

This is only one style of Roman blind and many other variations are possible. The ridge pockets can be made separately from the lining and then sewn on after the lining has been attached to the front fabric. Alternatively, the Roman blind can be left unlined, in which case the pockets for wooden stiffening are made either from folds in the fabric, or separately, using other fabric which is sewn onto the back afterwards. The pockets can even be placed on the front of the blind, made either in the same material or in a contrasting one. Kits for making a soft-folded version of the Roman blind, made with tapes instead of laths, are available.

For a less bulky look, the wood stiffening at the bottom of the blind can be omitted, to leave a finished edge hanging down. Alternatively, only the ridge at the very bottom of the blind is stiffened to make the folds softer and more bunched up.

◀ *A lovely, crisp white and brown linen Roman blind filters the light from the window. An attractive contrasting border has been added to the edges of the blind and finished with neatly mitred corners. The bottom of the main part of the blind has been decorated with a simple embroidered capital 'A', inspired by the engravings of Albrecht Dürer.*

Roller and Austrian blinds

Making a roller blind

To make a roller blind it is easiest to buy ready-stiffened fabric and a special kit (see pages 68 and 71). (If you choose to use your own fabric, you will need to treat it with a fabric stiffener. Iron the fabric before you do this.) The roller has a spring fitted into one end and is sawn to the required length before a second fitting is hammered into place. The kit also includes two brackets designed to take each end of the roller, which can be fixed either to the wall above the window or to the sides of a reveal.

Screw the brackets to the wall, the slotted bracket to the left, 3cm (1¼in) down from the top of a recess to allow for the thickness of the rolled-up blind. When fitting outside a recess, or to a window without one, position it 5cm (2in) above and out to each side.

Cut the fabric to the width of the roller, excluding fixtures, and if necessary join widths using flat seams. Use a right angle and a long wooden measure to ensure cutting is perpendicular with the sides and cut the fabric perfectly straight, with the weave.

Assuming the batten for the bottom of the blind is 25 x 5mm (1 x ¼in) thick, make a 4 cm (1½in) hem on the wrong side of the fabric and sew this in position with a zigzag stitch to create a pocket for the batten. Cut the batten to the correct length: it needs to be slightly shorter than the width of the blind, by approximately 1cm (⅜in), so that it does not show. Slide the batten into the pocket and slip stitch the ends. Attach the pull-cord holder to the wrong side of the batten (the same side as the hem).

Cut the roller to fit the brackets and hammer the other fitting into the sawn end. Draw a guideline along the length of roller, perpendicular to the ends, if it does not already have one. Position the fabric right side up and the roller on top with the spring to the left so that the top edge meets the guideline on the roller. Tape it to the roller to keep it steady and tack or staple the fabric to the roller.

Roll up by hand and slot into the brackets, right-hand end first. Pull the blind down to check the spring tension, rewinding by hand if necessary to increase the tension.

Making an Austrian blind or pull-up curtain

An Austrian blind is made like a conventional curtain, except for the finish to the heading and the system of rings and screw eyelets fixed at the back. (For a list of requirements see page 71). The description here is for separate rings but Austrian blind tapes can be used instead.

Depending on the weight of the fabric, the blind's heading can be attached to a hanging batten (also known as a heading board) with either Velcro or special Austrian blind track. The track has cord holders which line up above the cords.

For lightweight blinds, use a hanging batten and Velcro. Peel apart the two halves of Velcro and attach the stiff half across the front of the hanging batten with tacks or staples. Special Velcro heading tape, which gathers up in the same way as normal heading tape, but has Velcro instead of pockets, is also available. (For measuring up and determining fabric quantity, see page 70.)

Make up the blind as for an unlined curtain (see page 57), with leadweight tape in the hem if you want, and attach a fringe or other edging, if you are having one, to the back of the hem. The bottom edge looks more finished with a substantial trimming, like a deep fringe. When the blind is pulled up, this looks pretty against the light; when let down, it gives the bottom edge weight and definition.

To make a lined blind, sew the fabric and lining right sides together round three sides, catching in any fringe or trim between the layers as you stitch. Trim and turn right sides out, press and sew up the fourth side.

If not using special Velcro heading tape, sew on traditional heading tape to the top. Most heading tape types are suitable, but pencil pleats are recommended. Next, fold the blind vertically at evenly spaced intervals, about 60cm (2ft), where you want your scallops to be. The folds mark the positions for the rings. Bear in mind that an Austrian blind looks better with an odd number of swags rather than an even number, and the outermost rings on each side should be placed about 5cm (2in) from the edges.

Making a roller blind

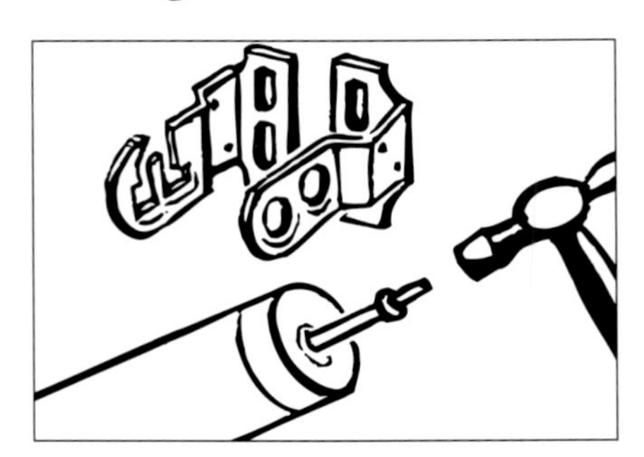

1 A roller blind kit comes with two wall brackets. Trim the roller to length and insert a fitting into the cut end.

2 Make a hem along the bottom and sew with a zigzag stitch. Insert the batten and slip stitch the ends closed.

3 The pull-cord holder is attached to the wrong side of the hem with two small screws.

4 The top edge of the blind is fixed to the roller with tacks or staples so that it hangs completely straight.

Sew the small rings at intervals on the back, making sure each row aligns. Note that when attaching the rings to a lined blind, you will need to catch some of the threads from the front fabric as well as the lining. If you are making a blind that retains its ruching when down, you will also have to attach a ring to the cords in the pulley system in order to stop the blind dropping fully at a certain point.

Sew the other half of the Velcro to a strip of matching fabric, or lining fabric, a little larger than the heading. Gather up the heading to the width of the finished blind, and attach the back of this Velcro/ fabric strip over the heading tape, turning in the edges. Make sure when sewing the Velcro to the fabric back that it will be at the correct height to attach to the Velcro on the hanging batten, i.e. at or very near the top of the blind.

Screw the eyelets into the bottom of the batten, one corresponding to each row of rings on the back of the blind plus an extra one on the side where the cords will hang down, as for a Roman blind (see pages 72–73). Fix the batten above the window, checking the horizontal with a spirit level. Fix the cleat to the window architrave or the wall.

Tie long cords to each of the bottom rings in each row and thread them up through the rest of the rings above them. Attach the blind to the hanging batten, and thread all the cords up through the eyelets and along to one side. Cut the cords to the same length, thread them through a drop weight and knot them.

▲ *This pull-up blind combines some of the features of a Roman blind and some of an Austrian blind: it is stiffened at the bottom, which means the blind lifts straight, not in festoons, but the folds are not sharpened with battens or dowelling, so it folds and crumples softly as it is pulled up.*

Making an Austrian blind

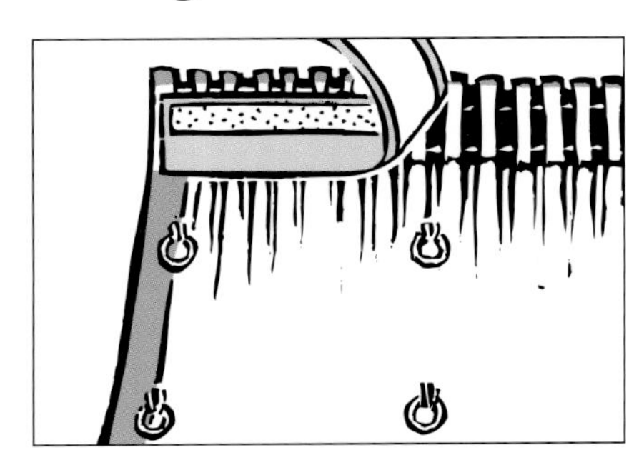

1 *Sew the rings onto the blind, aligning them in both directions. Slip stitch Velcro to the heading tape.*

2 *Fix the blinds onto the heading board, and thread up the cords through the rings and screw eyelets.*

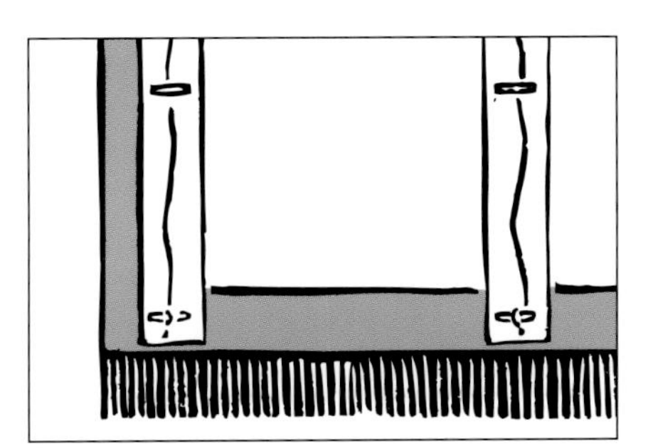

3 *Alternatively, special tapes with integral loops may be used. Take care to align the loops across the blind.*

Non-fabric blinds

▶ *Rattan blinds, slung across the glass roof of a garden room, give welcome shade and echo the natural texture and colour of the plaited grass rug on the floor beneath.*

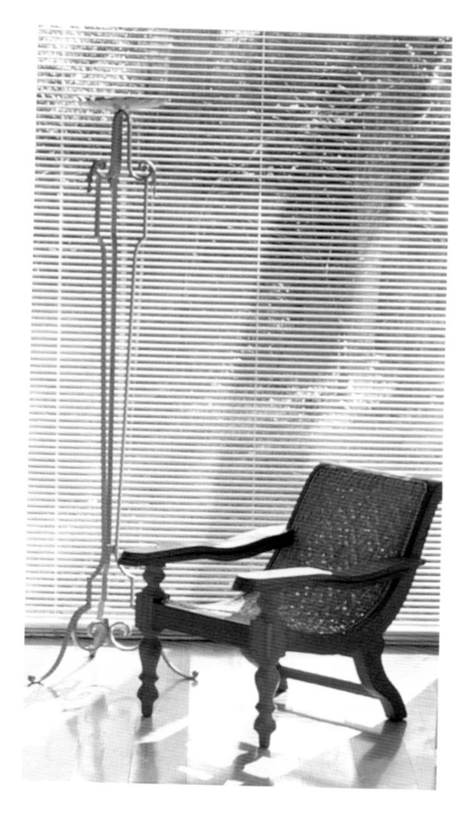

▲ *A massive louvred Venetian blind, made from aluminium alloy strips, filters the bright sunlight at a huge plate-glass window and provides a geometric background for an uncluttered space. The blind's neutrality and plain lines allow the interesting items of furniture, both traditional and modern, to feature without distraction.*

Blinds are made in a number of non-fabric materials. Bamboo, wooden slats, paper, metal and plastic blinds are available to suit all types of interior design styles. Some work on a simple roll-up principle which means they can be a little bulky when rolled up. Others are variations of the Venetian blind mechanism which pulls up neatly to the top of the reveal. The great advantage of this type of blind is that when down they can be adjusted to allow different amounts of light through at the touch of a cord.

Ready-made blinds are sold in a number of standard sizes, and in addition many types can be made up by suppliers to particular measurements and colours. Prices vary according to the materials used and the amount of work involved in making them up. Pleated paper, for example, can be among the cheapest, while metal Venetian blinds or those made with wooden slats can cost as much as fully lined curtains.

Paper

Made from pleated paper, these blinds keep their folds even when they are let down. They fit into the window reveal and so can be used in combination with curtains. They are easy to dust. Some have holes punched through them. Paper blinds are cheap to buy and are available in a wide range of colours.

Cane

Blinds made from whole or split cane either roll up or fold in pleats. They do not screen light completely but are useful in rooms where strong sunlight needs to be moderated, creating a pleasing filtered effect. At night, when a light is switched on, they are virtually see-through from outside. Privacy can be improved, however, by lining them with a simple panel of plain fabric. Make it slightly shorter than the blind and several centimetres narrower on each side, then glue or sew it to the cane across the top at the back. The lining will roll or fold up with the blind when the cord is pulled.

Wood

Blinds can be made from wooden slats, about 5cm (2in) wide, held equal distances apart and controlled by tapes. Adjusting the angle of the slats controls the amount of light the blind allows into a room. The wood may be left natural or stained or painted in any colour. Pinoleum blinds are thin wood strips woven with widths of cotton which diffuse sunlight in a pleasing way; but like split bamboo blinds, however, they can be seen through at night.

Plastic

Plastic strips can be used in the same way as wooden slats. Available in a range of colours, they are easy to wipe clean and therefore useful for kitchens and bathrooms, where soiling can be a problem.

Metal

Usually aluminium alloy strips, these are constructed into blinds in much the same way as wood slats and are traditionally known as Venetian blinds. They are available in a wide range of colours and finishes, including a mirror, striped or graduated finish. Perforated slats are also available to let some light through when the blind is fully closed.

Vertical louvre blinds

Vertical louvre blinds are suspended vertically from a track and linked at the bottom by a chain. They may be made of wood or synthetic flexible strips but are most commonly made of stiffened strips of fabric, often with a textured weave and usually 9–13cm (3½–5in) wide. Usually standing from floor to ceiling, they are drawn like curtains and are useful for shielding large picture windows or patio doors. The amount of light they let through is controlled by adjusting the angle of the louvres.

▲ *This blind is made from primed canvas bought at a theatrical supplier, and rolled around a length of wooden dowelling, but it could just as well be made from paper, with the edges reinforced against tearing. The natural-fibre rope is of a type available at any good DIY store.*

Stockists and suppliers

CURTAIN AND BLIND ACCESSORIES

Arthur Beale
194 Shaftesbury Avenue
London WC2H 8JP

John Lewis
Oxford Street
London W1A 1EX

FABRICS

Baumann Fabrics
41 Berners Street
London W1P 3AA

Colefax and Fowler
110 Fulham Road
London SW3 6RL

Designer's Guild
271 and 277 King's Road
London SW3 5EN

MacCulloch & Wallis Ltd.
25–26 Dering Street
London W1A 3AX

Osborne & Little
304–308 King's Road
London SW3 2HP

Pierre Frey
253 Fulham Road
London SW3 6HY

Pongees
28–30 Hoxton Square
London N1 6NN

Timney Fowler
388 King's Road
London SW3 5UZ

V. V. Rouleaux
10 Symons Street
London SW3 2TJ

PAINTS, STAINS AND VARNISHES

Brats
281 King's Road
London SW3 5EW

Brodie & Middleton
68 Drury Lane
London WC2

Cornelissen & Son Ltd.
105 Great Russell Street
London WC1B 3RY

Crown Berger Europe
P.O. Box 37
Crown House, Darwen
Lancashire BB3 0BG

Dulux
ICI Paints
Wexham Road
Slough
Berkshire SL2 5HD

Farrow & Ball Ltd.
Uddens Trading Estate
Wimborne
Dorset BH21 7NL

J.W. Bollom
13 Theobalds Road
London WC1X 8FN

Nutshell Natural Paints
Hamlyn House
Buckfastleigh
Devon TQ11 0NR

Paint Library
5 Elyston Street
London SW3 3NT

Paint Magic
116 Sheen Road
Surrey TW9 1UR

AUSTRALIA

Architectural & Design Centre
664 Botany Road
Alexandria
NSW 2015

Dulux Australia
McNaughton Road
Clayton
Victoria 3168

Home Hardware
414 Lower Dandenong Road
Braeside
Victoria 3195

McEwans
387–403 Bourke Street
Melbourne
Victoria 3000

NEW ZEALAND

Ven Lu-Ree Blind Service
11 Botha Road
Penrose
Auckland

Kresta
59c Carbine Road
Mt. Wellington
Auckland

Luraflex Window Fashions
22 Burminghan Drive
Riccarton
Christchurch
and
49 Hutt Road
Petone
Wellington

Window Treatments
19 Mandeville Street
Christchurch
and
726 Great South Road
Penrose
Auckland

SOUTH AFRICA

Art and Graphics Supplies
169 Oxford Road
7B Mutual Square
Rosebank
Johannesburg

Crafty Supplies
32 Main Road
Claremont
Cape

Home Warehouse
Johannesburg (Edenvale)
Dick Kemp Street
Meadowdale

Universal Paints
Randburg
24 Hendrick Verwoerd Drive
Cnr Dalmeny Road
Linden

JAPAN

Loving Design Center
Shinjuku Park Tower
3-7-1, Nishi-Shinjuku
Shinjuku-ku
Tokyo 163-10

Index

A

accessories, curtain 41
Austrian blinds 47, 68, 69, 70, 71, 74-5

B

blackout lining fabric 47
bleaches, woodwork 12, 27
blinds 45, 47, 66-77
brocade 47
brushes 3, 16-17, 32, 33
buying fabrics 44

C

calico 44
cane blinds 77
car paints 11, 29
carpets, paint spill on 32
casement windows 6, 21, 35
chemical paint strippers 13, 14, 15
chintz 45
cleaning up after painting 32
colour choices
  curtains 37, 44-5, 46, 56
  paintwork 6, 11
combing 19
  combs 16
cotton, embroidered 44
curtains 36-9
  accessories, poles, tracks 40-3
  fabric choices 44-7, 56
  making 48-61

D

damask 47
detachable curtain linings 59
doors 6, 10-17, 19, 22-9
  door furniture 34-5
dragging 19
draped fabric (curtains) 55

E

equipment
  for blind making 71
  for curtain making 49
  for paint finishes 11, 15, 16-17
escutcheons 34
espagnolettes 35
estimating quantities
  blind making 70
  curtain making 44, 48-9
  paints 16

F

fabrics
  choice for blinds 69
  curtain choices 37-9, 44-7, 56
  for door-coverings 28
  see also making
faux curtain poles 40
faux paint finishes 16, 24-5
festoon blinds 68
finger plates 34-5
finishes for woodwork (non-paint) 26-8
floors, paint spill on 32
floral prints 45
flush doors 6, 22-3, 24-5
French-polished wood 14
French windows 35
frosted glass 30-1
furniture, door and window 22, 34-5

G

gingham 45
glass 9
  decorative effects for 30-1
  painting around 20-1, 23
  see also windows

H

handles, door 34
headings, gathered (curtains) 52-5
hinges 35
hold-backs 64-5
hot-air guns 11, 12-13, 15

I

Indian crewelwork 39, 46
interlined curtains 47, 61

J

jacquard 45

K

kilim print (fabric) 46
knobs, door 22, 34
knotting solution 12, 15

L

lace 44, 56
lambrequins 44, 63
latches and locks 34
leather door-coverings 29
liming woodwork 27
linen curtain fabrics 44, 56
linings, curtain 39, 47, 58-61
  unlined curtains 56-7
locked-in curtain linings 60-1
loose-lined curtains 39, 58-9
louvre blinds, vertical 77

M

Madras cotton 45
making
  blinds 70-5
  curtains 48-61
masking tapes 20-1
measuring up *see* estimating quantities
metal
  blinds 77
  door fittings 22, 35
  facings for doors 29
  surfaces, painting 11, 14-15, 18
metallic-coloured spray paint 11, 29
milium (thermal lining) 47
mortise latches 34
mouldings, preparation of 13, 15
muslin 56

N

new wood, preparing 12
no-sew curtains 55

O

oiling woodwork 14, 26

P

padded doors 28, 29
painted glass 31
painting techniques *see* using paints
paints
  choice of 10-11, 18
  problems with 32-3
  using 11, 18-25, 31
paint shields 20-1
paint strippers 13, 14, 15
paisley 45
panelled doors 6, 22, 24-5
paper blinds, pleated 77
papering doors 28
patterned fabrics 44-6
pelmets 39, 47, 62-3
plastic blinds 77
pleating curtains *see* headings, gathered
plush 47
poles, curtain 40, 42-3, 48
portières 35
preparing surfaces for paint 12-15
Provençal prints 45
pull-up curtains 47, 68, 70, 71, 74-5
putty, checking 12

R

rattan blinds 76
'repeats', fabric pattern 49
rim latches 34
roller blinds 67-8, 69, 70, 71, 74
Roman blinds 47, 66, 68, 69, 70-3
rubber rockers 16, 19

S

sash windows 6, 21, 35
shavehooks 13, 15
sheers 56
sheet metal facings for doors 29
shutters 7-8, 21
skirting boards 23
special paint effects 16-17, 19, 24-5, 30-1
stained glass 31
stains for woodwork 11, 26, 27
stripping woodwork 12-14
swags and tails 62-3

T

tartan 46
textiles *see* fabrics
thumb latches 34
tie-backs 42, 64-5
tie-on curtains 55
toile de Jouy 45
tools *see* equipment
tracks, curtain 40-1, 43, 48
trimmings, curtain 39, 47

U

undercoats 18, 19, 32
unlined curtains 56-7

V

valances 41, 63
varnishes 11, 26, 27
velvet 47
veneers, wood 14
Venetian blinds 77
voile 44

W

waxing woodwork 14, 26-7
windows 6-9, 10-17, 19, 20-1, 26
  window furniture 35
  see also glass
wood bleaches 12, 27
wood blinds, slatted 77
woodgraining effects 19
wood stains 11, 26, 27
woodwork finishes (non-paint) 11, 26-8

Acknowledgments

The publisher would like to thank the following photographers and organizations for their kind permission to reproduce the photographs in this book.

1 Jan Baldwin/Options/Robert Harding Syndication; **2-3** Paul Ryan (Designer: Jason McCoy)/International Interiors; **4** Deidi von Schaewen; **5** Jerome Darblay; **6** Jan Baldwin (Andrew Mortada); **6-7** Simon McBride; **7** *above* Sølvi Dos Santos; **7** *below* Simon McBride; **8** Paul Ryan/International Interiors; **8-9** Albert Roosenburg/v t Wonen; **9** Nicolas Tosi (Stylist: C. Ardouin)/Marie Claire Maison; **10** John Miller; **11** Hotze Eisma; **12** Albert Roosenburg; **13** Hotze Eisma; **14** Polly Wreford/Homes & Gardens/Robert Harding Syndication; **14-15** Trevor Richards/Homes & Gardens/Robert Harding Syndication; **16** Francis Hammond; **17** Michael Mundy (Wilkinson); **18** Fritz von der Schulenburg/ (Adelheid Gowrie) The Interior Archive; **19** Hotze Eisma; **20** Richard Felber; **21** John Hall; **22** Henry Wilson (Celia Lyttleton)/The Interior Archive; **23** Richard Bryant/Arcaid; **24** Albert Roosenburg; **25** Jean Pierre Godeaut (Lisa Lovatt Smith); **26-27** David Phelps; **27** Dominque Vorillon; **28** *above* Simon Brown (Justin Meath Baker); **28** *below* Eric Morin; **29** Fritz von der Schulenburg/ The Interior Archive; **30** John Hall (Architectonica); **31** Henry Wilson (Ian Dew)/The Interior Archive; **32** John Miller; **33** Albert Roosenburg/v t Wonen; **34** *above* Gilles de Chabaneix (Stylist: M.Kalt)/Marie Claire Maison; **34** *below* Alexander van Berge; **34-35** Peter Woloszynski/The Interior Archive; **35** *above* Fritz von der Schulenburg/The Interior Archive; **35** *below* Marie–Pierre Morel (Stylist: J. Borgeaud)/Marie Claire Maison; **36** Marie–Pierre Morel (Stylist: C. Peuch)/Marie Claire Maison; **37** Ray Main; **38** *above* Henry Wilson (Ian Dew)/The Interior Archive; **38** *below* Nicolas Tosi (Stylist: J.Borgeaud)/Marie Claire Maison; **39** Polly Wreford/Homes & Gardens/ Robert Harding Syndication; **40** *above* James Merrell/Homes & Gardens/ Robert Harding Syndication; **40** *below* Henry Wilson (Ashley Hicks)/The Interior Archive; **40-41** Gavin Kingcome/Homes & Gardens/ Robert Harding Syndication; **41** *above* Nicolas Tosi (Stylist: J. Borgeaud)/Marie Claire Maison; **41** *below* Ray Main; **42** Tim Clinch/ The Interior Archive; **43** Polly Wreford/ Country Homes & Interiors/Robert Harding Syndication; **44** *above* Marie–Pierre Morel (Stylist: C. Peuch)/Marie Claire Maison; **44** *below* Jacques Dirand/Maison & Jardin; **44-45** Trevor Richards/Homes & Gardens/Robert Harding Syndication; **45** *above* Sanderson; **45** *below* Henry Wilson (Stephan Ryan)/The Interior Archive; **46** Fritz von der Schulenburg (David Bennett)/The Interior Archive; **46-47** *above* Christopher Drake/Country Homes & Interiors/Robert Harding Syndication; **46-47** *below* Jacques Dirand/Maison & Jardin; **47** Trevor Richards/Homes & Gardens/Robert Harding Syndication; **48** Paul Warchol; **49** *above* Jan Baldwin/Options/Robert Harding Syndication; **49** *below* Todd Eberle; **50** Jacques Dirand/Maison & Jardin; **51** Andreas von Einsiedel/Homes & Gardens/Robert Harding Syndication; **52** Christopher Drake/Homes & Gardens/Robert Harding Syndication; **53** Jacques Dirand/Maison & Jardin; **54** Christopher Drake/Country Homes & Interiors/Robert Harding Syndication; **55** Brigitte/Camera Press; **56** Fritz von der Schulenburg (Paula Navone)/The Interior Archive; **56-57** Debi Treloar/Homes & Gardens/Robert Harding Syndication; **58** Tom Leighton/Elizabeth Whiting & Associates; **59** Fritz von der Schulenburg (Mimmi O'Connell)/The Interior Archive; **60** Ray Main; **61** Jacques Dirand/Maison & Jardin; **62** Christopher Drake/Homes & Gardens/Robert Harding Syndication; **63** Hotze Eisma; **64** A. Gelberger/Maison Française/Agence Top; **65** John Hall; **66** Otto Baitz/Esto; **67** *above* Fritz von der Schulenburg (Architect: Nico Rensch)/The Interior Archive; **67** *below* Christian Sarramon; **68** Laura Ashley; **69** Peter Woloszynski (A.Parlance)/The Interior Archive; **70** John Hall; **71** Henry Bourne/ World of Interiors; **72** James Mortimer/The Interior Archive; **73** Christophe Dugied (Stylist: M.Bayle)/Marie Claire Maison; **75** Dominque Vorillon; **76** Henry Wilson (Christopher Davies)/The Interior Archive; **77** *above* Jean–Francois Jaussaud; **77** *below* Trevor Richards/Homes & Gardens/Robert Harding Syndication.